Aoife Smullen 4A6

Fishamble: The New Play Compan~
pre

RATHMINES ROAD

by Deirdre Kinahan

Rathmines Road previewed at the Civic Theatre, Tallaght,
as part of Dublin Theatre Festival on 4 October 2018,
before opening at the Abbey Theatre, Dublin, on the
Peacock Stage, on 9 October 2018.

Cast

Sandra	Karen Ardiff
Eddie	Charlie Bonner
Linda	Janet Moran
Ray	Enda Oates
Dairne	Rebecca Root

Production Team

Director	Jim Culleton
Set and Costume Designer	Maree Kearns
Lighting Designer	Kevin Smith
Sound Designer	Carl Kennedy
Fight Director	Ciaran O'Grady
Voice Director	Andrea Ainsworth
Hair & Make-up	Val Sherlock
Fishamble Production Manager	Marie Tierney
Abbey Theatre Production Manager	Cliff Barragry
Fishamble Stage Manager	Steph Ryan
Abbey Theatre Stage Manager	Anne Kyle
Fishamble Assistant Stage Manager	Sarah Purcell
Dramaturg	Gavin Kostick
Assistant Director*	Karen Stanley
Fishamble Production Coordinator	Ronan Carey
Fishamble Producer	Eva Scanlan
Abbey Theatre Producer	Jen Coppinger
Fishamble Marketing	Chandrika Narayanan-Mohan

*UCD and Gaiety School of Acting placement, as part of Fishamble's theatre company-in-association partnership

About Fishamble: The New Play Company

Fishamble is an Olivier Award-winning, internationally acclaimed Irish theatre company, which discovers, develops and produces new work, across a range of scales. Fishamble is committed to touring throughout Ireland and internationally, and does so through partnerships and collaborations with a large network of venues, festivals and non-arts organisations.

Fishamble has toured its productions to audiences in Ireland as well as to England, Scotland, Wales, France, Germany, Iceland, Croatia, Belgium, Czech Republic, Switzerland, Bulgaria, Romania, Serbia, Turkey, Finland, USA, Canada, New Zealand and Australia.

Fishamble and Pat Kinevane won an Olivier Award for *Silent* in 2016, when it was presented at Soho Theatre. Other awards for Fishamble productions include Scotsman Fringe First, Herald Angel, Argus Angel, 1st Irish, The Stage, Adelaide Fringe Best Theatre, Dublin Fringe, EMA, In Dublin, Forbes' Best Theater, Stage Raw LA, and Irish Times Theatre Awards, as well as Writers Guild of Ireland/ZeBBie and Stewart Parker Trust awards for many of its playwrights. Fishamble's living archive is in the National Library of Ireland.

Fishamble is at the heart of new writing for theatre in Ireland, not just through its productions, but through its extensive programme of Training, Development and Mentoring schemes. These currently include A Play for Ireland, the New Play Clinic and Show in a Bag, which is run in partnership with Dublin Fringe Festival and Irish Theatre Institute. Each year, Fishamble typically supports 60% of the writers of all new plays produced on the island of Ireland, approximately 55 plays per year.

'Fishamble puts electricity in the National grid of dreams'
Sebastian Barry

'a global brand with international theatrical presence' *Irish Times*

'Ireland's leading new writing company' *The Stage*

'forward-thinking Fishamble' *New York Times*

'excellent Fishamble... Ireland's terrific Fishamble' *Guardian*

fishamble.com | facebook.com/fishamble | twitter.com/fishamble

Fishamble is funded by The Arts Council, Dublin City Council and Fundraising Fellowship Dublin.

Its international touring is supported by Culture Ireland.

Fishamble's recent and current productions include

- *Before* by Pat Kinevane in association with the Strollers Network (2018)

- *Rathmines Road* by Deirdre Kinahan in co-production with the Abbey Theatre (2018)

- *Drip Feed* by Karen Cogan in co-production with Soho Theatre (2018)

- *GPO 1818* by Colin Murphy to mark the bicentenary of the GPO (2018)

- *Haughey | Gregory* by Colin Murphy in the Abbey Theatre, Mountjoy Prison, Dáil Éireann, and Croke Park (2018)

- *Maz & Bricks* by Eva O'Connor on national and international tour (2017–18)

- *Forgotten*, *Silent* and *Underneath* by Pat Kinevane (since 2007, 2011 and 2014, respectively – 2018) touring in Ireland, UK, Europe, US, Australia and New Zealand

- *On Blueberry Hill* by Sebastian Barry on national and international tour (2017)

- *The Humours of Bandon* by Margaret McAuliffe (2017–18) on national and international tour

- *Charolais* by Noni Stapleton (2017) in New York

- *Inside the GPO* by Colin Murphy (2016) performed in the GPO during Easter

- *Tiny Plays for Ireland and America* by 26 writers (2016) at the Kennedy Center, Washington DC, and Irish Arts Center, New York, as part of Ireland 100

- *Mainstream* by Rosaleen McDonagh (2016) in coproduction with Project Arts Centre

- *Invitation to a Journey* by David Bolger, Deirdre Gribbin and Gavin Kostick (2016) in co-production with CoisCeim, Crash Ensemble and Galway International Arts Festival

- *Little Thing, Big Thing* by Donal O'Kelly (2014–16) touring in Ireland, UK, Europe, US and Australia

- *Swing* by Steve Blount, Peter Daly, Gavin Kostick and Janet Moran (2014–16) touring in Ireland, UK, Europe, US, Australia and New Zealand

- *Spinning* by Deirdre Kinahan (2014) at Dublin Theatre Festival

- *The Wheelchair on My Face* by Sonya Kelly (2013–14) touring in Ireland, UK, Europe and US

Fishamble Staff

Jim Culleton (Artistic Director), Eva Scanlan (General Manager), Gavin Kostick (Literary Manager), Chandrika Narayanan-Mohan (Marketing and Fundraising Executive), Ronan Carey (Office and Production Coordinator)

Fishamble Board

Tania Banotti, Padraig Burns, Elizabeth Davis, Peter Finnegan, Doireann Ní Bhriain, Vincent O'Doherty, John O'Donnell, Siobhan O'Leary, Andrew Parkes (Chair)

Acknowledgements

Thanks to the following for their help with this production: Rachel West and all at the Arts Council; Ray Yeates and all at Dublin City Council Arts Office; Willie White, Maria Fleming, Stephen McManus and all at Dublin Theatre Festival; Michael Caven and all at the Civic Theatre; Laura MacNaughton, Aoife McCollum and all at the O'Reilly Theatre; all at 3 Great Denmark Street; Tracy Martin; Jane Koustas; Katie Shea; all those who have helped since this publication went to print.

Thanks to Lynda Sheridan, Toryn Glavin, Gordon Grehan, TENI, Paul Lucas, David Luff at Soho Theatre, Nina Steiger and Jacob Sparrow at the National Theatre, Ruth McGowan at Dublin Fringe Festival, Amy Rowan, Trans Creative, Lisa McNulty and Rachel Karpf at The Womens' Project, Rachael Gilkey at Irish Arts Center, Peter Daly, Mary Murray, and Aisling O'Sullivan for their help during the play's development process.

Fishamble wishes to thank the following Friends of Fishamble & Corporate Members for their invaluable support:

Alan & Rosemary Ashe, ATM Accounting Services, Mary Banotti, Tania Banotti, Doireann Ní Bhriain, Conor Braiden, Business to Arts, Breda Cashe, Maura Connolly, John & Yvonne Healy, Gillie Hinds, Monica McInerney, Stuart Mclaughlin, Ger McNaughton, Sinead Moriarty, Pat Moylan, Dympna Murray, Liz Nugent, Lisney, Vincent O'Doherty, Nora Owen, David & Veronica Rowe, Mary Stephenson, Patrick Sutton, and Tesco Finest. Thank you also to all those who do not wish to be credited.

ABBEY
THEATRE
AMHARCLANN
NA MAINISTREACH

About the Abbey Theatre

Inspired by the revolutionary ideals of our founders and our rich canon of Irish dramatic writing, our mission is to imaginatively engage with all of Irish society through the production of ambitious, courageous and new theatre in all its forms. We commit to lead in the telling of the whole Irish story, in English and in Irish, and we affirm that the Abbey is a theatre for the entire island of Ireland and for all its people. In every endeavour, we promote inclusiveness, diversity and equality.

Is é ár misean, faoi inspioráid idéil réabhlóideacha ár mbunaitheoirí agus ár gcanóin shaibhir scríbhneoireachta drámatúla de chuid na hÉireann, ná dul i dteagmháil go samhlaíoch le sochaí uile na hÉireann trí amharclannaíocht mhisniúil uaillmhianach nua de gach cineál a léiriú. Táimid tiomanta don cheannródaíocht i dtaca le scéal iomlán na hÉireann a insint, sa Bhéarla agus sa Ghaeilge, agus dearbhaímid gur amharclann í an Mhainistir d'oileán iomlán na hÉireann agus dá mhuintir uile. Déanaimid, i ngach iarracht dár gcuid, an ionchuimsitheacht, an ilchineálacht agus an comhionannas a chur chun cinn.

abbeytheatre.ie

Biographies

Deirdre Kinahan | Playwright

Deirdre Kinahan is an award-winning playwright. She is an elected member of Aosdána, Ireland's association of outstanding artists, Literary Associate with Meath County Council Arts Office and has served as a board member for the Abbey Theatre, Theatre Forum Ireland and the Stewart Parker Trust. Deirdre's work is translated into many languages, published by Nick Hern Books and produced regularly in Ireland and on the international stage. In 2018 Deirdre has new work at the Old Vic London (*Renewed* with Julie Walters), the Abbey Theatre Dublin (*The Unmanageable Sisters* – a new version of *Les Belles-Soeurs* by Michel Tremblay), Fishamble Theatre Company/Abbey Theatre (*Rathmines Road*), Meath County Council on Tour (*Me & Molly & Moo*, a play for children), Solas Nua, Washington (*Wild Notes*), Penatabus Theatre Company UK (*Crossings*) and Draiocht Dublin (*House*). Deirdre also has a number of other writing projects in development for 2019/2020. Plays include: *Rathmines Road, Crossings, The Unmanageable Sisters, Wild Sky, Spinning, Halcyon Days, Bogboy, Moment, Hue & Cry, Melody, Maisy Daly's Rainbow*. For radio: *Bogboy* (RTÉ) & *A Bag on Ballyfinch Place* (BBC). Agent Representation: Lily Williams, Curtis Brown, London. Leah Hamos, Gersh, New York. 'A ferociously funny and unexpectedly shattering writer'– *London Metro* on *MOMENT* 2011.

Jim Culleton | Director

Jim Culleton is the artistic director of Fishamble: The New Play Company. For Fishamble, he has directed productions which have toured throughout Ireland, UK, Europe, Australia, New Zealand, Canada and the US. His productions for Fishamble have won over a dozen Irish and international awards, including an Olivier Award for *Silent*. He has previously directed *Reading the Decades, Bookworms, Shush*, and *Down Off His Stilts* for the Abbey Theatre, as well as Fishamble's *Forgotten, Silent, Underneath* and *The Music of Ghost Light*, at the Abbey. He has also directed for companies including Woodpecker/the Gaiety, 7:84 (Scotland), Project Arts Centre, Amharclann de hÍde, Tinderbox, The Passion Machine, The Ark, Second Age, RTÉ Radio 1, The Belgrade, TNL Canada, Dundee Rep Ensemble, Draíocht, TCD School of Drama, CoisCéim/Crash Ensemble/GIAF, RTÉ lyric fm, Origin (New York), Vessel (Australia), and Symphony Space Broadway/Irish Arts Center (New York). Jim has taught for NYU, NUIM, GSA, Uversity, The Lir, Notre Dame, Villanova, TCD and UCD. For Fishamble, he most recently directed *Maz & Bricks* by Eva O'Connor in Edinburgh, and will next direct *Before* by Pat Kinevane on national tour, and *On Blueberry Hill* by Sebastian Barry in New York and on national tour.

Karen Ardiff | Sandra

Karen Ardiff was born in Dublin and graduated from the Samuel Beckett Centre in TCD. Karen most recent screen appearances include: the Oscar-nominated *Brooklyn*, directed by John Crowley, as well as RTÉ's *Acceptable Risk*. Other previous film and television includes: *The Bookshop* (Isabel Coixet); *Noble* (nominated for several international awards and three IFTAs); *A Terrible Beauty…* (Tile Films) as well as *Evelyn*. Karen most recently appeared on stage in the highly successful show *The Unmanageable Sisters* on the Abbey stage in the leading role of Rose. Other recent stage credits include: *Inside the GPO* (Jim Culleton, Fishamble); *Normal* (Maisie Lee, WeGetHighonthisCollective); *Angela's Ashes* (Thom Sutherland, Bord Gáis Energy Theatre); *Oedipus* (Wayne Jordan, Abbey Theatre); *Peer Gynt* (Lynne Parker, Rough Magic – Irish Times Best Supporting Actress nomination); *Threepenny Opera* (Wayne Jordan, The Gate Theatre); *Steel Magnolias* with Mischa Barton (The Gaiety Theatre); and *Love in the Title* (Abbey/international tour – ESB/Irish Times Best Actress Award). Work with other companies includes: *The Colleen Bawn* (Bedrock – Irish Times Best Supporting Actress nomination); *The Stuff of Myth* (Crazy Dog Audio Theatre & Lane Productions) and *Helene Hannf in 84 Charing Cross Road* (Andrews Lane Theatre – Irish Times Best Actress nomination for both). Karen has also performed in numerous radio dramas including: *Duet* (Newstalk), *Tempting Faith* and *Greed is Good* (BBC4).

Charlie Bonner | Eddie

After graduating from Trinity College Dublin, Charlie Bonner has worked with most theatre companies in Ireland north and south for over 25 years including *Whereabouts* and *Shorts* with Fishamble, and *Philadelphia Here I Come, Good Evening Mr. Collins, Monkey, Melonfarmer, Macbeth, Observatory, Living Quarters, The Shaughraun, Toupees & Snare Drums* and *Portia Coughlan* with the Abbey, and companies including the Gate and Lyric theatres, Prime Cut, Verdant Productions, Livin Dred, Pan Pan, Red Kettle, Corcadorca, Field Day and Second Age amongst others. Film and television includes: *Zoo, Maze, The Devil's Doorway, Childer, Rebellion, Red Rock, Omagh, The Tudors, The Race, Starfish, Proof, Fair City* and *The Crush*.

Janet Moran | Linda

Janet Moran is an actor and playwright based in Dublin. Selected theatre work includes: *Ulysses, The Plough and the Stars, Juno and the Paycock* (National Theatre, London/Abbey Theatre co-production), *Shibari, Translations, No Romance, The Recruiting Officer, The Cherry Orchard, She Stoops to Conquer, Communion, The Barbaric Comedies, The Well of the Saints* and *The Hostage* (Abbey Theatre); *Swing, Haughey | Gregory* and *Spinning* (Fishamble); *Car Show, Dublin by Lamplight, Everyday, Freefall* and *Desire Under the Elms* (Corn Exchange Theatre Co). Other theatre includes: *The Weir, Pineapple, Xaviers, Royal Supreme, Her Big Chance, Unravelling the Ribbon, Dancing at Lughnasa, Playing from the Heart, Guess Who's Coming for the Dinner, All's Well That Ends Well*. Film and television work includes: *Trivia, Love/Hate, Love is the Drug, T* (RTÉ), *Dublin Oldschool, The Bailout, The Butcher Boy, Breakfast on Pluto, Milo, Minim Rest, Bono and My Ex, Moll Flanders, Nothing Personal, Volkswagen Joe* and *Quirke* (BBC). Writing credits include: *Swing* (international tour) and *A Holy Show* (Peacock Theatre).

Enda Oates | Ray
Enda Oates has a long association with Fishamble going back to 1999 when he appeared in Joseph O'Connor's *True Believers* at Andrew Lane and its subsequent Irish tour and its run at The Tricycle, London. Other Fishamble productions include: *The Plains of Enna* by Pat Kinevane, *Whereabouts*, and *Pilgrims in the Park* by Jim O'Hanlon. Enda is delighted to be returning in Fishamble's 30th year with this show. At the Abbey Theatre, credits include: *Curse of the Starving Class, The Corsican Brothers, Big Maggie, Colours, The Devil's Disciple, St. Joan, A Child's Christmas in Wales* and *Blinded by the Light* amongst others. He played Prospero in Corcadorca's open air production of *The Tempest* for Cork's Year of Culture in 2006 and Shylock in *The Merchant of Venice* for Second Age. Other theatre: *Philadelphia Here I Come* (Lyric/Gaiety Theatre); *The Field* (Gaiety); *Jacques Brel is Alive and Well* (Noel Pearson Productions/Gate Theatre); *Uncle Vanya* (Field Day); *The Plough and the Stars* (Young Vic); *Studs/Buddleia* (Passion Machine Project Arts/Donmar Warehouse); *Juno and the Paycock* (Gate Theatre/ Broadway); *The Ha'penny Bridge* (Point Theatre); *The Country Boy, The Chastitute* (Ed. Farrell Prod); *Further than the Furthest Thing* (Hatch Theatre, Project Arts). In 2015 Enda won Best Actor IFTA for his role as Pete Ferguson in the RTÉ production *Fair City*. Radio credits include: *The Hit List* and *Domestic Robots* written and directed by John Boorman *Charlois, Ma* (Elaine Murphy); *Goodnight Irene* (Jennifer Johnston) and *The Thriller Series, Grave Danger* amongst others. Film and television includes: *Secret Scripture* (Voltage Productions); *Striking Out* (Blinder Films); *Glenroe, Upwardly Mobile* (RTÉ); *Tri Sceal, Wrecking the Rising*(TG4); *Moone Boy* (Sky 1); *Raw, Rebellion 2* (RTÉ); *Val Falvey, Superhero* (Grand Pictures); *The Bailout* (TV3); *Stardust* (Media Films); *Ordinary Decent Criminal* (Littlebird); *An Everlasting Piece* (Dreamworks); *Eden* (Samson Films) and *Damo & Ivor* (Granno Productions).

Rebecca Root | Dairne
Rebecca Root is best known for playing Judy in BBC Two's ground-breaking comedy series *Boy Meets Girl*. Other screen credits include: *The Sisters Brothers, Colette, The Danish Girl, Flack, The Romanoffs, Moominvalley, Hank Zipzer, Doctors, Hollyoaks, Celebrity Mastermind, Casualty, The Detectives, Midsomer Murders*, and *Keeping Up Appearances*. Theatre credits include: the award-winning play *Trans Scripts* at the Edinburgh Festival Fringe in 2015, revived in 2017 at American Repertory Theater in Cambridge, Massachusetts. Other theatre includes: *The Bear / The Proposal* at the Young Vic, and *Hamlet* at the Gielgud Theatre. Rebecca is also a voice and speech coach, working chiefly with trans clients. She is patron of the charities *Liberate* (Jersey) and *Diversity Role Models*, and is a passionate advocate for LGBT visibility, equal rights and societal acceptance. For further information please visit www.rebeccaroot.co.uk

Maree Kearns | Set and Costume Designer

Maree Kearns is a set and costume designer whose work spans across theatre, musicals, dance and opera. *Rathmines Road* marks her third time working with Fishamble having previously designed *Maz and Bricks* and *Invitation to a Journey* (CoisCéim, Crash Ensemble and GIAF co-production). She has also designed two other Deirdre Kinahan plays: *These Halcyon Days* (Edinburgh Fringe First 2013) and *Moment* for Landmark/Tall Tales. Some of her most recent designs include: *Class* for Inis Theatre in association with the Abbey Theatre (Edinburgh Fringe First 2018); *Giselle* for Ballet Ireland and *The Wizard of Oz* at the Cork Opera House. Other work includes: *Annie the Musical & Prodijig the Revolution* (Cork Opera House); *Agnes, Pageant & Faun/As You Are* (CoisCéim Dance Theatre); *Vampirella, Opera Briefs 2018, 2016 & 2014* for R.I.A.M; *Monsters, Dinosaurs & Ghosts* (Peacock Theatre); *Desire Under the Elms* (Corn Exchange); *These, Zoe's Play & Far Away From Me* (The Ark); *Hamlet, King Lear, Romeo and Juliet, Macbeth* and *Dancing at Lughnasa* (Second Age); *Moll & Anglo the Musical* (Verdant Productions); *Plasticine* (CorcaDorca); *A Winter's Tale, Three Winters, In the Next Room, Scenes from the Big Picture* and *Troilus and Cressida* (The Lir); *The Dead School & Observe the Sons of Ulster Marching Towards the Somme* (Nomad Theatre Network; Irish Times Best Set Designer 2009). Maree is the MFA Stage Design Course Director in the Lir Academy of Dramatic Art in Dublin.

Kevin Smith | Lighting Designer

Kevin Smith trained at The Samuel Beckett Centre, Trinity College Dublin. This is the third time he has designed a Deidre Kinahan premiere, having previously designed *Spinning* with Fishamble, *These Halcyon Days* with Tall Tales & Landmark Productions which won a Fringe First in Edinburgh, and *Wild Sky* with Ten42 Productions. His other theatre design credits include: *Class* with Inis & Abbey Theatre which recently won a Fringe First in Edinburgh. Also *Monsters Dinosaurs & Ghosts* (Abbey Theatre, Peacock Stage); *Rhinoceros* (Blue Raincoat Theatre Co); *Scenes from the Big Picture, In The Next Room, Three Winters, La Ronde* (The Lir); *Barney Carey Gets His Wings* (Barnstorm); *Beowulf The Blockbuster* (Pat Moylan Productions); *The Family Hoffmann Mystery Palace* (The MAC & Cahoots NI); *Driving Miss Daisy, Moll* (Gaiety); *The Faerie Thorn, Puckoon* (Big Telly). His dance design credits include: *12 Minute Dances* (Liz Roche Co.); *Coppelia* (Ballet Ireland); *Manifesto* (Maiden Voyage). He also designed *An Outside Understanding* with Croí Glan which was nominated for Best Design (Absolute Fringe). Kevin's opera design credits include: *Vampirella, Saints & Sinners* and *Clori Tirsi é Fileno* with RIAM. and *Flatpack* (Ulysses Opera) which was nominated for an Irish Times Best Opera Production.

Carl Kennedy | Sound Designer

Carl Kennedy trained at Academy of Sound in Dublin. He has previously worked with Fishamble: The New Play Company on *Maz and Bricks* by Eva O'Connor, *Inside The GPO* by Colin Murphy and *Little Thing Big Thing* by Donal O'Kelly, all directed by Jim Culleton. He has worked as a composer/sound designer with venues and companies including: The Abbey, The Gaiety, Decadent, ANU Productions, HOME Manchester, Prime Cut, Theatre Lovett, HotForTheatre, Rough Magic, The Lyric Theatre Belfast, Gúna Nua, Loose Canon, Peer to Peer, Siren, Broken Crow, Randolf SD and Theatre Makers. He has been nominated three times for the Irish Times Theatre Award for Best Sound Design. He also composes and sound designs for television, radio and video games. Game titles include: *Curious George, Curious about Shapes and Colors, Jelly Jumble, Too Many Teddies, Dino Dog* and *Leonardo and His Cat*. Television credits include: sound design for *16 Letters* (Independent Pictures/RTÉ) and SFX editing and foley recording for *Centenary* (RTÉ). For RTÉ Jr radio, he was recently composer/sound designer/sound editor for *Mr Wall* by Dee Roycroft, which has been shortlisted for an IMRO Radio Award 2018 in the drama category.

Gavin Kostick | Dramaturg

Gavin Kostick, as Literary Manager at Fishamble, works with new writers for theatre through script development, readings and a variety of mentorship programmes. For Fishamble, Gavin is particularly proud of his work on *Show in a Bag, The New Play Clinic, Tiny Plays for Ireland* and *A Play for Ireland*. Gavin is also an award-winning playwright. He has written over twenty plays which have been produced nationally and internationally. Recent favourite works include: *Invitation to a Journey* and *The End of the Road; This is What we Sang* for Kabosh; *Fight Night, The Games People Play* and *At the Ford* for RISE, and the Libretto for *The Alma Fetish* for Raymond Deane and Wide Open Opera. As a performer he performed Joseph Conrad's *Heart of Darkness: Complete*, a six-hour show for Absolut Fringe, Dublin Theatre Festival and The London Festival of Literature at the Southbank. His work in all areas has received many national and international awards.

Eva Scanlan | Producer

Eva Scanlan is the General Manager and Producer of Fishamble: The New Play Company. Current and recent producing work includes: *On Blueberry Hill* by Sebastian Barry; Fishamble's award-winning Pat Kinevane Trilogy on tour in Ireland and internationally; *The Humours of Bandon* by Margaret McAuliffe; *Maz and Bricks* by Eva O'Connor; *Inside the GPO* by Colin Murphy; *Tiny Plays for Ireland and America* at the Kennedy Centre in Washington DC and the Irish Arts Centre in New York, and *Swing* by Steve Blount, Peter Daly, Gavin Kostick and Janet Moran on tour in Ireland, the UK, and Australia. Eva produces *The 24 Hour Plays: Dublin* at the Abbey Theatre in Ireland (2012–present), in association with the 24 Hour Play Company, New York, and has worked on The 24 Hour Plays on Broadway and The 24 Hour Musicals at the Gramercy Theatre. Previously, she was Producer of terraNOVA Collective in New York (2012–2015), where she produced *terraNOVA Rx: Four Plays in Rep* at IRT Theater, the soloNOVA Arts Festival, the Groundworks New Play Series, *Woman of Leisure and Panic* (FringeNYC), *P.S. Jones and the Frozen City*, among other projects.

A Reckoning

It strikes me that Ireland is going through something of a reckoning at present. Recent referendums on civil liberties, tribunals into political ethics and corruption, inquiries into clerical and institutional abuse, all signal an enormous shift in Irish thinking. The iron grip of Catholicism and stifling absolutism of class and convention are beginning to dissipate, and to my mind that is a good thing. Unfortunately there are many areas in which we still fail and fail spectacularly. In *Rathmines Road*, I want to explore our collective response to accusations of rape and sexual assault, and our complete failure judicially, socially and culturally, to negotiate the dreadful consequences of these crimes. So I decided to place a victim of sexual assault into a situation where he/she can confront that abuse in a public way and then watch each character shift and spin in the ways described by survivors. I wanted to try to feel what it is like to be blamed for inciting the very crime committed on you. What it is like to be constantly doubted. What it is like to be perpetually judged and labelled by that crime. What it is like to see your story, your truth and your dignity stolen from you by the people affected by that accusation – and how quickly the response becomes not about you but about them, and how your accusation affects them. I wanted to try to feel what it is like to disappear – disappear into an abyss where every social cultural and judicial reflex conspires to silence, to shame and to deny…YOU.

It was in writing the play that I began to understand how the failure of our response is often governed by gender and the cultural expectations associated with gender. *Boys will be boys* remember and *good girls don't get drunk or don't go into bedrooms at parties unless they are willing to be sexually assaulted or raped.* It sounds absurd. I have to say I have trouble even writing that sentence, but how many daytime-chat-show callers, opinion-column writers, neighbours, solicitors or indeed deluded bishops give air to the notion that a victim of sexual assault is in some way culpable – if not *asking for it*? It is extraordinary how control of the narrative of a crime is often removed from the person at the centre of it, then reshaped to fit the needs of those around them. The perpetrator of sexual assault rarely admits their crime, rarely sees it and in most cases is never forced to answer for it. And so you will see how each character in *Rathmines Road* attempts to take control of the story and recreate it in some way to suit their sense of themselves. You will see how some characters lie, lie constantly, and lie first to themselves because the capacity for human denial never ceases to amaze me, particularly when backed up by silence. Silence sits at the heart of *Rathmines Road* because, unfortunately, silence remains the go-to response for survivors, their abusers and ourselves. Silence means we might not have to respond at all.

Thank you.

Deirdre Kinahan
September 2018

RATHMINES ROAD

Deirdre Kinahan

This play is for my two amazing daughters
Síobhra & Sadhbh O'Farrell

Characters

SANDRA, *forty-five, originally from Wicklow – living in London for twenty-four years*
RAY, *forty-eight, from London*
DAIRNE, *forty-five, originally from Wicklow – living in UK/NYC for twenty years*
LINDA, *forty-two, from Wicklow*
EDDIE, *forty-six, from Dublin*

Timeline

Present: 2018

Incident on Rathmines Road: 1993

This text went to press before the end of rehearsals and so may differ slightly from the play as performed.

Scene One

We are in an old-fashioned sitting room. The lighting is low.
A couple are entwined, having just had sex on the couch.

RAY. God… I'm getting too old for this!

SANDRA. No you're not. You're amazing.

RAY. No you're amazing.

SANDRA. You know I love you, don't you, Ray.

You know I love you more than anything.

You and Séan and Emma. You are everything to me.

Everything.

EVERYTHING.

RAY. Who are you shouting at?

SANDRA. I don't know.

Everyone maybe.

Everything.

RAY. Are you sure you're all right?

SANDRA. Yes.

RAY. Are you crying?

SANDRA. No.

RAY. Are you sure… you look like you're crying?

SANDRA. No I'm not… I'm fine. I'm honestly fine.

RAY. Okay. But what was going on with you this evening?

SANDRA. What?

RAY. When the others were here?

SANDRA. Nothing!

RAY. Nothing?

SANDRA. Do you mind moving… I just want to fix my dress.

He rolls off her and on to the floor. He starts to pull up his trousers.

RAY. Of course. Sorry.

I don't know why sex feels so illegal in here.

SANDRA. It's still my mother's sitting room.

RAY (*looking at a photo frame*). And there she is looking right out at us.

SANDRA. Sorry, Mammy…

SANDRA *wipes away a tear. She is both laughing and crying.*

RAY. Sandra?

SANDRA. I'm fine… honestly.

RAY. You are crying?

SANDRA. It's just…

Jesus.

Poor Mammy.

This was her good room.

RAY. Oh dear…

SANDRA. I know.

He puts his arm around her.

RAY. Are you sure you're okay?

SANDRA. Yes.

RAY. I've never... never seen you ask anyone to leave before... what was it?

SANDRA. I don't know...

RAY. Have you changed your mind?

You don't want to sell?

SANDRA. No no, it's not that.

RAY. What then?

SANDRA. I don't know.

I don't...

She gets up.

RAY. It's emotional?

SANDRA. Yes, exactly, it's emotional and I couldn't... I just couldn't cope with them poking around and I couldn't... not with the evening... sorry.

RAY. You don't have to apologise to me.

SANDRA. No, no I know I don't.

RAY. And it's only natural you're attached to the place. We really don't have to sell...

SANDRA. Maybe we don't.

Or maybe we do...

RAY. It's pretty here. It could make a nice holiday home?

SANDRA. Shouldn't you want to go on holidays to your holiday home? I'm sorry, Ray, I'm just... I'm not myself.

RAY. Well, whatever you want, love.

Whatever you decide I'll row in with it.

Auctioneers are ten to a penny.

SANDRA. I know they are.

RAY. We can contact another company when you're ready.

SANDRA. Yes. That's exactly what we can do.

RAY. I never thought it was a good idea to ask a friend anyway.

SANDRA. You never said?

RAY. Didn't I?

SANDRA. No, and I wouldn't call Linda a friend, Ray. I just knew her from school, knew her sister from school.

She takes a deep breath and has to hold on to the sideboard.

RAY. What is it?

SANDRA. Nothing. I'm okay. I'm okay.

He approaches her.

She swings around violently.

RAY *is startled.*

RAY. Christ!

SANDRA. What?

RAY. You look terrified.

SANDRA. Do I?

RAY. Yes… what is it, love, what's wrong?

SANDRA. Nothing. Nothing's wrong.

I'll be all right.

She takes a deep breath again.

RAY. Is it a panic attack?

SANDRA. Yes… yes, that's what it is… a panic attack.

RAY. Do you need to sit down?

SANDRA. No.

RAY. You haven't had one of them for years?

SANDRA. I know. I haven't, have I?

I think it's just all this…

RAY. Well, let's forget all this.

We'll just go home, Sandra.

SANDRA. Yes. Go home.

RAY. And we can sell the place online if needs be.

SANDRA. Yes. Online.

RAY. We'll go home.

We'll go home tomorrow?

A day early.

SANDRA. Yes… that's a great idea, Ray.

I want to go home.

RAY. The kids will be delighted…

SANDRA. Yes they will.

And let's use it, Ray.

Let's use your day off work to take them somewhere…

A hotel or something.

With a swimming pool.

RAY. Whatever you like.

SANDRA. They love a hotel.

RAY. Sure, whatever you want, Sandra.

Are you feeling better now?

SANDRA. A little bit.

RAY. Great. Don't scare me like that.

SANDRA. Sorry.

RAY. Can I hug you now?

SANDRA. Yes please.

RAY. Has it stopped?

Your heart?

SANDRA. Not entirely!

She forces a laugh.

Thank God.

RAY. Thank God.

SANDRA. I'll be fine, Ray.

I promise I'll be fine.

RAY. Good.

I'll make tea then, shall I?

SANDRA. Yes. Perfect.

RAY. And we'll bring it up to bed?

SANDRA. Yes, yeah.

RAY. Come on so.

SANDRA. In a minute…

Just a minute…

RAY. You want to stay here?

SANDRA. Just for a minute, I'll make the tea and follow you up.

RAY. But I'll be freezing in that bed all by myself.

SANDRA. Get under the duvet and call the kids.

That's what I do, then everything feels all right.

RAY. What?

SANDRA. Nothing. Honestly, Ray, I'm fine. I'll be fine.

RAY. Okay but you'll be up?

SANDRA. Yes… Yes… I'll be up.

I just want to catch my breath.

Call me when you get through to the kids.

RAY. Okay.

SANDRA. Okay, Ray.

RAY *exits*.

SANDRA *stands where she is*.

She lifts up her hand and looks at it. It is shaking.

She grips her arms around herself.

Christ.

Jesus Christ.

*She starts to walk around the room, shaking out her hands,
flexing, breathing*.

Fuck you. Fuck you.

Fuck you, Eddie Dunne.

She smacks her hand to her mouth at the sound of his name.

She almost shrieks.

Oh God.

She flops onto the couch.

Beat.

What the fuck just happened here tonight?

*A hoover appears into the room all by itself. It switches on
almost like a challenge*. SANDRA *looks at it*.

Scene Two

SANDRA *goes over to the hoover, takes it by the handle*
gingerly and then slowly starts hoovering the room. Lighting
indicates a shift in time. We are now back to earlier that
evening. The doorbell rings. SANDRA *stops hoovering. Her*
demeanor is very different. She checks her watch. She goes to
the door leaving the room empty. We hear voices as she and her
guest approach.

DAIRNE *enters ahead of* SANDRA.

DAIRNE. Oh wow… you haven't cleared it?

SANDRA. What?

DAIRNE. The house.

SANDRA. No? Should I?

DAIRNE. Usually… before a sale.

SANDRA. Oh…?

DAIRNE. Jesus this room is like a time capsule…

SANDRA. Is it?

   I mean, yes, I suppose it is.

   Isn't yours?

   Your mother's?

DAIRNE. God no, haven't you been in?

SANDRA. No. I met her in the village last time I was over…

DAIRNE. I thought she said that you had called.

SANDRA. No. Should I? I suppose I should.

   We… I. I'm rarely home.

DAIRNE. So she says.

SANDRA. Yeah.

   I think that that was over a year ago?

   When I met her?

DAIRNE. She went crazy after Daddy died – fitted kitchen, designer bathroom, gave the house a total makeover.

SANDRA. Really? Fair play to her.

DAIRNE. There's that much glass you can see nothing but yourself as you walk up the drive. She's been glued, you see, to the Nordic dramas...

SANDRA. Has she?

DAIRNE. Went on cruise and all to Oslo. Next thing is a hot tub in the garden.

SANDRA. Right!

DAIRNE. She said you were mad to see me!

SANDRA. Did she?

DAIRNE. Aren't you?

SANDRA. Yes.

  DAIRNE *laughs*.

DAIRNE. You were never a good liar, Sandra Byrne.

SANDRA. I'm not lying.

  It's great, it is great to see you.

DAIRNE. Mammy saw you arrive in this morning.

SANDRA. Did she? Jesus, I almost forgot how small Glenealy is.

DAIRNE. Never forget how small Glenealy is!

  Anyway she insisted that I call...

SANDRA. And I'm glad... I'm glad...

  Pause.

DAIRNE. So aren't you going to say anything?

  About me?

SANDRA. You?

DAIRNE. Yes.

SANDRA. No. No, your mother... or someone told me you that you had... transformed.

DAIRNE. Transformed?

SANDRA. Transitioned.

I'm sorry.

But you look amazing.

You do.

DAIRNE. You look good yourself.

SANDRA. Older?

DAIRNE. We're all older.

SANDRA. So what do I call you now?

DAIRNE. Dairne.

SANDRA. Dairne?

DAIRNE. Yes.

SANDRA. That's nice.

Not far from David.

DAIRNE. No not far from...

Pause.

SANDRA. Well.

DAIRNE. Well!

SANDRA. I don't know what I'm supposed to say now.

Are you happy?

...Did it hurt?

DAIRNE *laughs*.

DAIRNE. It's good to see you, Sandra.

SANDRA. Why?

DAIRNE. I hear you're doing really well over there… in London.

SANDRA. From who?

DAIRNE. From Mammy of course.

SANDRA. Of course.

Slight pause.

But when did you get back from the States?

DAIRNE. Two years ago.

SANDRA. Really?

DAIRNE. Yes.

SANDRA. For good?

DAIRNE. Yes for good.

I had enough of New York.

SANDRA. Did you.

DAIRNE. Yes. It's hard.

It can be a hard place.

SANDRA. What did you do over there?

DAIRNE. All sorts.

SANDRA. Theatre?

DAIRNE. Sometimes.

I thought I should come home after Daddy died.

SANDRA. Right.

I see.

Did he ever… your dad… did he ever know that you… transitioned?

DAIRNE. Yes, in a way… though I think he still considered it a phase.

SANDRA (*almost laughing*). Christ!

DAIRNE. We never got into the mechanics.

SANDRA. No.

DAIRNE. It was easier just to talk on the phone.

SANDRA. But what about when you came home? How did he manage that?

DAIRNE. I didn't come home. Not for years.

Mammy used to come over to me.

She was delighted at that stage. I was the girl she never had. The two of us used to go off on cruises… Bahamas… or maybe fly down to Florida.

SANDRA. Very nice.

DAIRNE. It was. Girls are much kinder to their mothers apparently.

SANDRA. She's gas.

DAIRNE. She is.

SANDRA. God when I think of all you had to put up with… all the fuss…

And now you're here.

DAIRNE. Yes. Now I'm here, large as life, in your front room.

SANDRA. Yes.

DAIRNE. First time in what?

Twenty, twenty-five years?

SANDRA. Not twenty-five?

DAIRNE. Almost twenty-five.

SANDRA. God...

Pause.

DAIRNE. You never wrote.

SANDRA. Didn't I?

DAIRNE. No. And I wondered.

I wondered how you were doing.

SANDRA. I was... I am... doing fine... thanks.

DAIRNE. So I see!

SANDRA. Yes.

...Did you write?

DAIRNE. Eh... no.

SANDRA *smiles.*

I'm loving Dublin now though.

SANDRA. Good for you.

DAIRNE. Thanks.

Slight pause.

Where are you living then... in London?

SANDRA. Molesey.

DAIRNE. Christ that sounds leafy!

Practically underground...

SANDRA *laughs again.*

And where is your handsome brother?

SANDRA. Brussels.

DAIRNE. Of course he is.

I bet he works for the UN or something?

SANDRA. He does.

Human Rights.

DAIRNE. Of course.

SANDRA. He's married now.

Three kids.

DAIRNE. Are you trying to hurt my feelings?

She smiles.

SANDRA. No.

Though I always hated that you fancied him instead of me.

DAIRNE. I know you did.

Slight pause.

So!

SANDRA. So?

DAIRNE. Is that wine?

SANDRA. Wine?

DAIRNE. On the sideboard.

SANDRA. Yes that's wine.

Would you like some?

DAIRNE. Yes please.

SANDRA *starts to lift the cork.*

Four glasses?

Are you expecting someone?

SANDRA. Just the estate agent.

DAIRNE. The estate agent is coming for drinks?

SANDRA. Yes, it's Suzie Levins' sister. Do you remember her?
    She was two years behind us at school. She's coming over to
    look at the place...

DAIRNE. Do you need me to go?

SANDRA. No, they won't be here for ages.

I just… I just want to hand it over, you know, hand the whole thing over.

DAIRNE. Why?

SANDRA. Because… because I'm busy.

I have a busy life.

DAIRNE. Great.

SANDRA. Yeah.

Anyway I'm all curious now.

DAIRNE. Are you?

SANDRA. Of course.

I mean… it's such a change yet…

DAIRNE. Yet…?

SANDRA. I'd know it's you.

Except maybe for the voice…

DAIRNE. The voice?

SANDRA. Or accent…

But I'd know your eyes.

I think I would always know your eyes.

Slight pause.

I never thought you'd come back to Ireland though… of all people!

DAIRNE. Sure I had to catch up with all the old gang.

SANDRA. You did!?

DAIRNE. Hardly! You know I hated them… hated everyone except you.

SANDRA. College was different.

DAIRNE. Yes, college was different.

Because no one gave a shit.

Here's to not giving a shit!

She toasts. SANDRA *joins her.*

They drink.

SANDRA. So what are you doing now?

In Dublin?

DAIRNE. I'm living with someone.

SANDRA. Are you?

DAIRNE. Yes. Pat. He's a nurse. He cycles, he cooks and he's fabulous. We're even thinking of getting married.

SANDRA. Well! Congratulations.

DAIRNE. Thank you. Who'd have thought it… in Ireland!

SANDRA. Yes. Yes. And what do you do?

DAIRNE. Do?

SANDRA. For work?

DAIRNE. I work in IT.

SANDRA. IT!?

DAIRNE. Software development.

SANDRA. Jesus how did that happen?

DAIRNE. I don't know really. I was doing a show in the States and one of the dancers… he had a brother… and we… well, we were together for a while and he had a software company… so I just…

SANDRA. Fell into it.

DAIRNE. Yeah.

SANDRA.... You always fell into things.

DAIRNE. Did I?

SANDRA. Yes.

DAIRNE. Anyway. I'm all conventional now.

SANDRA. Hardly!

She laughs.

DAIRNE *doesn't.*

There is the sound of someone coming in the front door.

Oh God... that's Ray.

You'll meet Ray.

He's my...

DAIRNE. Husband?

SANDRA. Yes.

My husband.

RAY (*entering*). Okay, love. I think I got everything. I decided to get a bottle of gin as well.

DAIRNE. I think I love Ray already.

RAY. Oh right you're here.

You must be Linda!

DAIRNE. No.

SANDRA. No. This is...

DAIRNE. Dairne.

RAY. Dairne?

SANDRA. We're old friends.

RAY. Really? Great to meet you.

They shake hands.

DAIRNE. You too.

SANDRA. He just popped in.

DAIRNE. I just popped in.

SANDRA. We haven't seen each other for years.

RAY. Right… okay.

Fantastic.

Well, I'm Ray!

I've just been out to get some supplies and one of these fire-log things!

SANDRA. Oh… that's a great idea, Ray.

RAY (*to* DAIRNE). To start a fire.

The place is bloody freezing

SANDRA. We tried the heating…

RAY. But there's an airlock or something.

He starts trying to light the log.

Best bet is one of these things I think.

DAIRNE. I just wonder if that might be wise?

RAY. Sorry?

DAIRNE. There might be birds up the chimney or something…

SANDRA. Oh?

RAY. Birds?

DAIRNE. Yes.

RAY. Doubt it, Dairne.

Should be fine.

Bit of atmosphere if nothing else.

DAIRNE. Sure. Bit of atmosphere.

RAY. Do you know, I might just hop up and change, I got drenched again!

DAIRNE. Bloody Ireland!

RAY. Eh… yes, yeah?!

DAIRNE. Go get dry, Ray.

RAY. I will. I will. Thanks…

SANDRA. Dairne.

RAY. Dairne.

He's gone.

DAIRNE. Well… he's not bad, not bad at all, Sandra Byrne.

SANDRA. Were you just flirting with him?

Flirting with my husband?

DAIRNE *laughs.*

DAIRNE. How long are you two married?

SANDRA. Twelve, no, fourteen years.

DAIRNE. Wow!

SANDRA. Is that good?

DAIRNE. That's long.

Kids?

SANDRA. Yes. Kids.

DAIRNE. One boy.

One girl?

SANDRA. What's that supposed to mean?

DAIRNE. Nothing…

SANDRA. I think that you're insinuating something.

DAIRNE. I'm not.

SANDRA. I know you.

DAIRNE. I'm only asking… honestly!

SANDRA. Okay!

One boy.

One girl.

Emma and Séan.

DAIRNE. Perfect.

SANDRA. See… you were insinuating something.

DAIRNE. I just knew it would all work out for you.

SANDRA. And?

DAIRNE. I'm glad!

I'm really glad, Sandra.

There's a ring on the doorbell. SANDRA *turns.*

SANDRA. What?

DAIRNE. That must be your estate agent!

SANDRA. It can't be… I've nothing done!

DAIRNE. Do you want me to answer the door?

RAY (*off*). They're early, Sandra!

SANDRA. I know.

RAY (*off*). Can you get the door?

SANDRA. No, I need to put this stuff away!

RAY (*off*). Okay I'll get it.

SANDRA (*to* DAIRNE). Stick that polish in the drawer, will you.

I'll be back in a minute.

She exits other direction to the front door (kitchen) and with the hoover.

We hear greetings being made out in the hall. RAY *and* LINDA *and* EDDIE *enter.*

DAIRNE *stands up.*

DAIRNE. Hiya!

LINDA. Oh hello!

RAY. This is Dairne. An old friend of Sandra's.

LINDA. Dairne?

DAIRNE. Sandra just went into the kitchen.

EDDIE. Hi there.

LINDA. This is Eddie, my husband.

EDDIE. Linda's husband.

DAIRNE. Lovely.

RAY. Great.

    So can I get you guys a drink?

DAIRNE. Sandra opened a bottle of wine...

RAY. Did she?

EDDIE. Yes please...

LINDA. Wine is perfect.

    SANDRA *comes in with a bowl of ice for gin and tonics.*

SANDRA. I'm so sorry I just popped into the kitchen.

LINDA. Sandra Byrne, look at you!

SANDRA. Hi Linda... Oooh hang on and I'll just put this stuff down...

LINDA. It's so great to see you...

SANDRA. Yes, thanks... thank you so much for coming round.

LINDA. I'm delighted.

    We're delighted.

Aren't we, Eddie?

This is Eddie, the hubby.

EDDIE *comes forward.*

EDDIE. Hi Sandra… what a lovely old place this is!

EDDIE *gives* SANDRA *a strong handshake.*

LINDA. It is, isn't it.

DAIRNE. Welcome to about 1980…!

RAY. Yes…!

LINDA. We call it 'character'! Nothing a good clear-out and lick of paint can't fix. And this room is just soooo cosy!

DAIRNE. It is, isn't it.

RAY. Would you rather a gin and tonic than the wine. Linda?

LINDA. No thanks. Ray.

DAIRNE. I might have a gin. Ray?

RAY. Oh sure… and you, Sandra?

SANDRA *doesn't answer.*

LINDA. So how old is the house?

SANDRA *doesn't answer.*

LINDA *smiles expectantly.*

Sandra?

SANDRA. Sorry…?

LINDA. How old is the house?

I know it looks sixties but the layout doesn't fit…

RAY. It was a farmhouse, wasn't it, Sandra? Originally? And then your dad added on…

SANDRA. Yes… Dad added on…

EDDIE. Regularly, by the looks of things!

Lots of flat roof!

RAY. Yes.

DAIRNE. A dead giveaway, is it, Linda?

LINDA. God yes... a lot of ad-hoc extensions were done in the seventies...

EDDIE. Usually without planning permission.

LINDA. And that can cause complications with the sale.

RAY. Oh dear...

LINDA. I'm not saying that it will in this case, Ray, but best to be forewarned. (*Coughs*.)

RAY. Oh... right... great.

EDDIE. Was it long in the family?

SANDRA *doesn't answer.*

RAY. Sandra?

SANDRA. Oh... yes... sorry... at least back to Granddad... it was my granddad's house.

LINDA. You have the deeds?

SANDRA. I do. We do.

LINDA. Super. I thought I might take all the documentation with me tonight. Then do the tour! So I know what we are talking about in terms of valuation.

RAY. Great... that sounds great, doesn't it, San?

SANDRA. Eh... yes... yeah.

LINDA. Because you two leave on – ?

RAY. Monday.

Can't let the kids kill their gran!

LINDA. No!

EDDIE. That wouldn't be very helpful!

LINDA. Ahhhhhhh God how old are the kids, Sandra?

> SANDRA *doesn't answer. She just stands motionless.*
> RAY *interjects, a bit perplexed by her behaviour.*

RAY. Emma is eleven.

> And Séan is seven.

LINDA. Gorgeous! You'll have to bring them over next time…
so we can meet them.

RAY. Yes… yes… they love a trip. They love it here… don't
they, Sandra?

SANDRA (*quietly*). Yes.

RAY. But we thought it better to focus on the business of the
house for this visit.

LINDA. Absolutely.

EDDIE. Get this albatross SOLD!

RAY. I suppose so…

LINDA. And is your brother happy to sell?

SANDRA. Yes.

RAY. Everything is in order on that front.

LINDA. Good… Wow, Eamon Byrne… My sixteen-year-old-
self would just die at the thought of being in his front room!
Eamon was the heart-throb round Glenealy, Ray!

DAIRNE. Yes he was.

LINDA. Oh… did you know him… Dairne?

DAIRNE. Vaguely.

LINDA. And where is he now, Sandra?

SANDRA. Brussels.

LINDA. Married and all?

SANDRA. Yes.

DAIRNE. Darn it!

LINDA *laughs politely.*

Slight pause.

SANDRA *hasn't moved from the back wall.*

EDDIE. So where are you from yourself, Ray?

RAY. London, well, London via Fanore.

We moved over when I was a kid.

EDDIE. Fanore County Clare?

RAY. Yes.

EDDIE. That's a lovely spot, isn't it, Linda.

I think we went surfing there once?!

LINDA. Yes we did.

Sweet little place.

RAY. Hungry little place.

EDDIE. And have you people there?

LINDA. A house?

RAY. No. No. They're all gone.

All in England now.

LINDA. Really!

EDDIE. Linda tells me you work in television, Ray?

RAY. Yes, I do.

LINDA. Very exciting!

RAY. Not really. I'm in the finance end.

Sandra is the creative in the family.

EDDIE. Really... are you, Sandra?

SANDRA *just stands rigid against the wall. There is a pause.*

RAY. Is everything okay, love?

SANDRA. No, no… Yes.

RAY. Are you sure?

SANDRA. Yes… I'm sure.

LINDA. Great.

Still, you must get to meet a lot of celebs?

RAY. Sandra does.

LINDA. Aren't you the dark horse!

No one round here knew you were in the BBC?!

SANDRA. I'm not in the BBC.

LINDA. Oh?

SANDRA. I work for a small production company.

DAIRNE. Writing?

SANDRA. Editorial.

DAIRNE. Well done.

LINDA. So, do you make programmes then for the BBC?

SANDRA. Sometimes…

RAY. Documentaries.

LINDA. Oooooooooooh!

EDDIE. And are you in that world, Dairne?

DAIRNE. Me? No.

EDDIE. So how do you two know each other then?

There is a slight pause.

RAY. College?

DAIRNE. Yes we went to UCD together.

EDDIE. Oh? What year?

LINDA. Eddie went to UCD.

EDDIE. Economics '90 to '95.

LINDA. Eddie teaches now.

EDDIE. Did the dip.

LINDA. He's Principal at Saint Ultans, that's the local secondary school.

SANDRA. Jesus!

LINDA. Sorry?

RAY. What's up...?

SANDRA. I just... I just... I think I put some samosas in the oven. I better... I better just go check on them.

LINDA. Oh but you shouldn't have gone to that trouble...!

SANDRA *exits.* RAY *looks confused.*

RAY. Right, well... more wine, anyone?

LINDA. Yes please.

EDDIE. I must say this chair is interesting.

LINDA. Very vintage.

EDDIE *sinks almost to floor level in a seventies-style wood and leather chair.*

DAIRNE. I think Sandra's dad was a bit of a DIY enthusiast.

RAY. Yes he was... did a lot of the work around the house...

DAIRNE. Even built items of furniture.

EDDIE. Ah...

RAY. As you see.

EDDIE. It's comfy… but a bit low…

He attempts to get out of it, then changes his mind.

LINDA. We can get rid of all the furnishings for you, Ray.

RAY. Great.

EDDIE. So do you guys come over regularly then?

RAY. No. Not really. Not since Sandra's dad died… but when the kids were born, of course.

LINDA. Of course!

EDDIE. And you're not tempted to hold on to the place at all?

Renovate? Invest?

RAY. No. Well, I thought we might at one stage but Sandra… I think life is busy enough in London.

LINDA. I'm sure it is. And best to sell then before it deteriorates.

RAY. Exactly.

EDDIE. Any further!

RAY. Okay… got it!

LINDA *coughs*.

LINDA. Is it just me or is it a bit smoky in here?

DAIRNE. I think it might be a bit smoky!

EDDIE. Could it be those samosas?

DAIRNE. Or that fire?

I wonder is it the fire, Ray?

RAY. God… it might be…

DAIRNE. You see it probably hasn't been cleaned in years…

EDDIE. Might be best to put it out.

RAY. Right. Good call. And how do I do that?

DAIRNE. Just throw something over it. It's only one of those logs.

LINDA. Because if it gets very hot… a lot of soot might come down.

EDDIE. Or the whole chimney go on fire.

RAY. Are you serious?

DAIRNE. Yes, just use that jug of water.

EDDIE. I'm sure I can help!

But he can't quite get out of the chair.

DAIRNE *throws a jug of water over the fire getting half of it on* EDDIE.

DAIRNE. Oh sorry, Eddie.

EDDIE. Not to worry…

Only a drop.

RAY *gives him an antimacassar to dry himself off with.*

LINDA. I might just open a window.

DAIRNE. Good idea.

SANDRA *returns with a tray of nibbles.*

RAY. Spot of bother here with the log, love.

SANDRA. Oh.

LINDA. There might be birds up there or something.

DAIRNE. Exactly.

SANDRA. Sorry about that.

LINDA. Not at all.

Old houses…!

EDDIE. Booby traps!

DAIRNE *goes to take the tray.*

DAIRNE. Well, I must say… these all look delicious.

LINDA. Don't they!

SANDRA. Thanks…

RAY. Aren't you going to sit down, love?

SANDRA. Of course.

Yes.

She doesn't.

EDDIE *makes a gallant effort to get up whilst holding his glass of wine.*

DAIRNE. I'll bring something over, shall I, Eddie?

EDDIE. Yes please!

RAY. And I'll top up the wine.

DAIRNE. Great idea, Ray.

LINDA. So… I told Suzie I was coming round to see you.

(*To* RAY.) Suzie is my sister.

SANDRA. Oh… did you?

LINDA. She's sorry she couldn't make it.

Exhausted.

She is expecting her third!

SANDRA. Really?

DAIRNE. Is that a baby?

LINDA. Of course it's a baby!

DAIRNE. Oh… right.

LINDA. And I think she's insane. That's three kids under eight, and she's over forty. She'll have to give up work!

DAIRNE. Wouldn't that be a bitch!

LINDA. Meaning?

DAIRNE. Meaning… I'd love to give up work.

EDDIE. And do you have children, Dairne?

DAIRNE. No.

RAY. Do you…

Yourself and Eddie?

EDDIE. We have two.

LINDA. Molly and Megan.

EDDIE. I'm surrounded!

DAIRNE. Well, lucky you, Eddie!

RAY. And do you teach girls… in your school?

EDDIE. I do… yes.

SANDRA *exclaims*.

EDDIE *keeps going*.

It's a mixed school.

Community. Well-rounded.

LINDA. But Eddie has high ambitions for it, don't you, Ed.

EDDIE. Of course! We have a great staff… highly motivated.

RAY. Excellent.

DAIRNE. These eggs are lovely, Sandra.

EDDIE. Aren't they…

LINDA. Very unusual.

DAIRNE. Devilled. Would you like another one, Eddie?

EDDIE. No, I'm fine, I might just hop up…

He gets caught in the chair and completely topples, wine and plate flying.

RAY. Oh crikey!

They all go to assist except SANDRA.

Are you all right?

LINDA. What happened!

EDDIE. I think it was the chair…

But I'm fine. Honestly… just…

DAIRNE. It's probably not used to that weight.

RAY. Antique…

LINDA. I don't think so!

Just a stupid crappy chair.

EDDIE. I'm okay, Linda…

RAY. Just watch that plate there, Linda…

LINDA. Oh…

LINDA *steps backwards onto the plate in her heels and twists on her ankle. She lets out a shriek.*

SANDRA. God!

RAY. It's all right… not a crisis.

LINDA. It's bloody sore. I think I might have twisted it.

EDDIE. Did you?

LINDA. I don't know.

RAY. Can you check Linda's foot? See if it's swollen?

SANDRA. Of course.

SANDRA *gets down on her knees.*

RAY. I'm really sorry about that, Eddie.

EDDIE. Not at all. Not at all.

He limps back over to the couch and sits beside LINDA. SANDRA *freezes.*

LINDA. I don't feel anything!

   Can you see anything?

   SANDRA *doesn't answer.*

   For God's sake, it's fine. I think it's fine.

RAY. No damage.

LINDA. No.

RAY. Great.

EDDIE. Yes.

   SANDRA *stands up and goes back to the wall.*

DAIRNE. Well!

   That was exciting!

   No one responds.

   Beat.

LINDA. So maybe I should see the house?

   I mean we have a babysitter but she likes to get home early.

EDDIE. Yes she does.

RAY. Of course.

   Of course.

   Sandra will show you around.

   Won't you, Sandra?

   SANDRA *shakes her head.*

LINDA. You won't show me around?

SANDRA. I'm just… I'm not sure…

RAY. Are you feeling all right?

EDDIE. Bit of a flu going… half the kids are out the last two
   days…

SANDRA. No, I'm fine… no, not fine.

Yes, not brilliant.

Would you mind?

RAY *looks at* SANDRA, *he is totally bemused.* SANDRA *shakes her head again. Music starts to fill the stage. It is muffled.* SANDRA *can hear it. It sounds like Nirvana ('All Apologies') or the Cranberries ('Zombie'). It is in her head. The others don't seem to notice it at all.*

Maybe… actually… yes… would you mind, Ray?

LINDA. Just a quick look around the rooms so that I can write a description?

RAY. Yes. Quick trip. No problem. I'll do it.

LINDA. You coming, Eddie?

EDDIE. Yes. Yes. I think I will.

EDDIE *starts knocking the walls like he is some kind of expert.*

RAY. Great.

Dairne?

DAIRNE. No.

RAY. Right… off we go… Kitchen and downstairs first I think.

They exit.

SANDRA. Fuck!

Fuck… fuck… fuck!

DAIRNE. What is it?

SANDRA. Jesus.

The music gets louder. SANDRA *sits down and starts to breathe in and out slowly… this is in a practised manner.* DAIRNE *goes over to her. She puts her hand on her shoulder.* SANDRA *startles, screams and jumps up.*

DAIRNE. Sorry, Jesus… what's wrong with you?

SANDRA. Fuck. Fuck.

DAIRNE. You said that already!

The music starts to fade.

SANDRA. It couldn't be.

It can't be.

It just can't be.

DAIRNE. What can't be?

SANDRA. This hasn't happened to me for years.

DAIRNE. What hasn't?

SANDRA. I used to… I used to think… I used to dream a lot.
Dream about them… see the faces… his face and hear the
music… a lot. But this is different. Jesus this is different. He's
here… it's him… I'm sure of it. He's one of them and he's in
the front room. Mammy's front room. Daddy's front room!

DAIRNE. Who?… Eddie?

SANDRA *exclaims and puts her hand to her mouth.*

What the hell is it?

SANDRA. What's her name?

DAIRNE. Whose name?

SANDRA. Her name… Linda's fucking name… her married
name… that's her business card on the table… look at it…
look at it will you… what does it say?

DAIRNE. It says Linda Levins.

SANDRA. She didn't change her name?

DAIRNE. I don't know…

SANDRA. She didn't change her name… but he's Eddie
Dunne, I'm sure of it.

She quickly draws in her breath.

Oh God… he's Eddie Dunne!

DAIRNE. Who's Eddie Dunne?

SANDRA. We've got to get him out.

Get them out of here.

I don't think I can hold it together.

DAIRNE. Why do you need to hold it together?

SANDRA. You're right.

You're right.

Why do I need to hold it together?

He's here in my house.

Mammy's house.

Jesus.

I can't believe it.

And he doesn't know me!

He doesn't even fucking know me!

DAIRNE. I'm sorry… I just… I've no idea what you're talking about, Sandra…

SANDRA. As soon as he came in.

I felt it. I knew it.

Oh God… I'm shaking.

I have the shakes.

This hasn't happened in years.

DAIRNE. Why are you shaking?

SANDRA. Or maybe it's you.

Is it you?

That's what I thought when I went out…

DAIRNE. Out where?

SANDRA. Into the kitchen.

You've thrown me. With your... with all this!

Or is it the wine?

Or the stupid chair?

DAIRNE. I don't know...

...I kind of loved the chair!

She laughs.

SANDRA *laughs too but it is a manic laughter.*

SANDRA. My heart. My heart...

It's racing.

Feel it.

She pulls DAIRNE*'s hand to her heart.*

Can you feel it?

DAIRNE. I can.

It's pumping!

SANDRA. Pumping.

Pumping.

That's what happens.

And I start to shake.

DAIRNE. Why?

SANDRA. Trauma... post-traumatic... trauma!

DAIRNE. From what?

SANDRA. Oh Christ, David...

DAIRNE. What?

LINDA *has entered.*

LINDA. David?

DAIRNE takes her hand away from SANDRA.

She smiles at LINDA.

DAIRNE. That was my name.

Years ago.

LINDA. Okay.

Sure.

She pauses.

Is everything okay?

SANDRA *doesn't answer.*

Okay, well, Ray has shown me around the house… and it's great… it's obviously in need of a refurb but we can advertise it that way… and I'm sure, given the location and the garden and the fact that you're not overlooked, I'm sure I can get you a good price.

SANDRA (*quietly*).…okay…

LINDA. So I might just go through these few questions and then Ed and I will…

EDDIE *and* RAY *return.*

EDDIE. Ed and I will what?

LINDA. Head off.

Because I'm not sure that Sandra's feeling too well.

SANDRA. I'm not…

I'm not feeling too well.

RAY. Oh…?

EDDIE. That's a shame.

SANDRA. So we won't bother with the questions because I'm not going… I'm not going to sell to you… with you. I'm,

I'm awfully sorry but I'd like you to go. I think you should go, Linda, if you don't mind because... because I'm just not feeling too well.

RAY. What?

SANDRA. Please please I'd really just like you to go... all to go!

LINDA. Jesus.

EDDIE. Okay not to worry. Selling the old place can be a bit stressful... we understand...

He moves towards SANDRA.

SANDRA. No! No! Don't come near me... don't...

She darts into the kitchen.

They all stand there, speechless.

Scene Three

SANDRA *returns. She stands and looks at the others for a beat... suddenly we spring backwards, repeating the following sequence exactly as played before.*

LINDA. So I might just go through these few questions and then Ed and I will...

EDDIE. Ed and I will what?

LINDA. Head off.

Because I'm not sure that Sandra's feeling too well.

SANDRA. I'm not...

I'm not feeling too well.

RAY. Oh...?

EDDIE. That's a shame.

SANDRA. Is your name Eddie Dunne?

EDDIE. What?

She almost shrieks it.

SANDRA. Eddie Dunne?

EDDIE. Eh… yes!

Again she almost shrieks.

There is a slightly shocked pause.

DAIRNE. I wonder if we know each other?

LINDA. I sincerely doubt it.

SANDRA. Oh God!

DAIRNE. Are you from around here, Eddie?

EDDIE. No.

RAY. Is everything all right, Sandra?

EDDIE (*uneasy*). And are you, Dairne?

LINDA. Yes I think Dairne's from just up the road.

David Burke, isn't it?

I remember now.

You were in Suzie's class too, now it all makes sense.

EDDIE. Well, I'm glad it makes sense to someone.

SANDRA (*quietly*). Eddie Dunne…

Eddie Dunne…

LINDA. You've had a sex change!

EDDIE. What?

LINDA. He's had a sex change!

RAY. What?

DAIRNE. No one calls it a sex change any more.

LINDA. It's all the rage.

RAY. What are we talking about?

LINDA. Trans.

DAIRNE. What did you say?

SANDRA (*quietly*). You were there, Eddie Dunne.

You were there all along.

RAY. Sandra?

SANDRA. He was there all along.

RAY. Who was?

SANDRA. He was.

Eddie Dunne.

EDDIE. What?

RAY. What on earth is going on?

SANDRA. And you don't even know me?

You don't even know me, Eddie Dunne.

EDDIE. This is getting a little uncomfortable.

LINDA. Yes, I agree.

Very uncomfortable. So I'll tell you what. We're going to leave, Ray. I think she's obviously… your wife… Sandra, she's obviously, you're obviously suffering from something, Sandra Byrne.

SANDRA. Look at me.

Look at me, you bastard.

EDDIE. Me?

SANDRA. Yes you. You bastard.

RAY. Sandra?

SANDRA. Rathmines Road... Rathmines Road.

It was you, wasn't it?

EDDIE. I've no idea?

LINDA. What is this...?

Eddie?

The music floods the stage again now. It is rhythmic. Lights start to flash.

SANDRA. We were at a club.

The Concorde.

And you were there.

I know it was you.

Eddie and Donal and Jay.

LINDA. How do you know Donal?

EDDIE. Shut up, Linda!

RAY. Who's Donal?

SANDRA. I'm sure.

I'm so horribly fucking sure.

Eddie and Donal and Jay.

RAY. Sandra? What's wrong? What's going on with you?

Please, love, you're not making any sense.

SANDRA. I feel sick.

EDDIE. She feels sick.

LINDA. She's off her bloody trolley... always was... and him!
I remember the pair of them now in school... weirdos...
I think they were even screwing.

RAY. What?

LINDA. Before he was gay.

Or before he was trans.

God knows.

Eddie, let's get out of here.

SANDRA. No.

LINDA. We've had enough of this!

SANDRA. He's not going.

He's got to hear.

Got to hear this.

LINDA. Hear what?

SANDRA. It was the last fling before the exams.

And you were there.

Weren't you, Eddie Dunne. You know you were.

But you weren't part of the usual crowd.

Different hair. Better shirts.

And we were dancing.

Back at the house.

And there was vodka.

E's.

The usual.

And Donal.

LINDA. What is it with Donal?

SANDRA. I don't know what I was doing.

To get so sexed, sexual while still dancing… still dancing with him on the floor.

But I wanted him.

And I think about that now.

I think about it all the time.

And wonder…

Was that the plan all along?

Was that how you did it…?

Or were you just watching?

Watching?

And it was *me* that made you decide…?

Think you could?

Think you could?

There is a very loud sound of a thud.

SANDRA *grabs her head.*

My head.

My head.

It hit the wall.

Do you remember, Eddie Dunne?

When you threw me on the floor.

LINDA. What is she saying?

RAY. Sandra?

SANDRA. Because all three of you came into the room.

All three of you.

And I didn't know.

I didn't see.

The whole thing was like a dream.

When he held me down.

When Donal held me down for you.

LINDA. This is monstrous…!

SANDRA. First Jay.

Wasn't it?

But he couldn't do it. He was too drunk.

And I could see him. Gagging, tugging. His hand on my
mouth so I couldn't scream.

Then his fist. His hands. Your hands. On my face and on
my... all over me...

LINDA. Stop this shit.

She needs to stop this shit.

SANDRA. Everywhere! You were everywhere. Pulling my hair.

And mauling.

Till you pushed me off the bed and on to the floor.

And I thought it was over.

And I nearly cried because it was over.

But then you.

You gently turned me.

And I wanted to cry.

Please Please No.

No, Eddie Dunne.

You don't want to do this.

You don't want to do this.

To me.

But you did.

And you smacked me into the wall.

So fast.

Not gentle now.

You broke my nose.

Broke my nose on the wall.

As you beat into me.

And still I couldn't scream.

I was lost.

In my throat.

In that moment.

And I know you remember.

I saw your face.

You looked me in the eye.

When you were finished.

When you took a swig of your beer.

And went back to the party.

And I know that you can see it now too.

You remember me.

LINDA. Like hell he does.

EDDIE. I wasn't…

I was never.

LINDA. Tell her, Eddie!

EDDIE. I was never on Rathmines Road.

SANDRA. You're lying.

He's lying, Ray.

RAY turns and punches EDDIE *in the face.*

It is a shock to everyone, including RAY.

LINDA. Jesus Christ!

RAY. Jesus Christ!

EDDIE. It wasn't me!

I'm telling you...

I've never.

I've never met her.

Never met this woman.

Never met you.

This is lunacy...

LINDA. It's lunacy all right.

And we're suing!

I'm suing!

You fucking animal!

How dare you!

How dare you hit my husband!

RAY *goes straight over and hits* EDDIE *again.*

EDDIE. Stop... stop it.

She's got it wrong.

It wasn't me...

RAY *hits him again.*

I swear!

It wasn't me.

RAY *hits him again. But they are weak ineffectual hits.*
LINDA *looks to* DAIRNE.

LINDA. Do something!

Do something!

He'll kill him...!

DAIRNE. I really don't think that he will.

LINDA *jumps on* RAY*'s back.*

LINDA. Hit him back.

Hit the bastard back, Eddie!

EDDIE. I can't...

RAY *staggers with* LINDA *still on his back.*

SANDRA *picks up a bottle.*

RAY. Sandra!

She smashes it over EDDIE*'s head.*

The entire stage goes black except a spotlight on SANDRA*'s face with her eyes closed.*

SANDRA. I close my eyes.

The most primal reflex.

The most childish reflex.

To close my eyes.

Close my eyes to the blood on my legs, on my face.

Close my eyes to the laughter still out there at the party.

Close my eyes to the voices that ask where I am going.

I just close.

Close up.

Close down.

Close.

Beat.

The lights come back up. The stage is empty except for SANDRA.

She sits on the couch.

She has her arms wrapped tightly around herself.

She is breathing in the same practised manner as earlier, trying to calm herself.

RAY *enters. He stands.*

RAY. They've left. They're gone.

SANDRA. Are you sure?

RAY. Yes. Almost took the front gate with them as they drove away.

SANDRA. Okay...

RAY. Are you okay?

SANDRA. No.

RAY. You know you could have killed him with that bottle?!

SANDRA. I wish I did.

RAY. She said that they are going to the police.

SANDRA. I'm going to the police.

RAY. What?

SANDRA. I should have gone years ago.

RAY. Sandra...

SANDRA. Yes?

RAY. Sandra.

How could you have kept this from me?

SANDRA. Stop...

RAY. How could you keep... how could you have kept that from me...?

SANDRA. No one knew.

RAY. No one?

SANDRA. No.

RAY. Why?

SANDRA. For Christ's sake, Ray!

RAY. Why?

SANDRA. Why are you shouting at me?

RAY. I'm not shouting at you.

You are shouting at me and I'm trying…

I'm just trying to understand what the hell… what just happened here?!

SANDRA. So am I.

RAY (*going over to her*)….Sandra.

She stands up quickly.

Jesus!

SANDRA. It's all right.

RAY. Is it? It doesn't feel all right…

SANDRA. He raped me.

Eddie Dunne raped me.

That's what happened.

That's what happened, Ray.

And Jay Blake.

All three of them.

No, not Donal.

But the other two.

At that party.

And I didn't want them.

I didn't know them.

I didn't know that they were there.

RAY. Fuck…

SANDRA. It was a game.

Some sort of student game they used to play…

I know it happened…

With others… to others…

I know.

It was all over the campus.

But I never… I NEVER said yes…

And I NEVER wanted them, Ray.

But they just did it anyway.

Did me anyway.

And then left me on the floor.

RAY. This… this is… fuck it's awful…

SANDRA. I know.

And I'm sorry.

RAY. Why are YOU sorry?

It's not YOU that should be sorry.

SANDRA. I couldn't

I could never tell, Ray.

I could never tell anyone ever.

You need to understand that.

I hope you understand that.

Because…

Because I couldn't bring it home.

Bring that home… here.

How could I?

When Mammy was already sick… with cancer… and we… the house… we were all in such a stupor with it… I… I was in a daze.

Please tell me that you understand that.

RAY. I do…

SANDRA. Because I was afraid.

Because it was at a party.

And I had been with Donal but only with him.

I didn't know the other two.

I didn't know that they were there.

You have to believe me…

RAY. Please, Sandra… please…

You don't have to say it all again…

SANDRA. But I do.

I do. Don't you see.

Or else it disappears.

And I almost don't believe it myself…

Even then.

Even at that time…

If it wasn't for the bruises… for my nose.

I had to go to the hospital for my nose.

RAY. You had to go to the hospital?

SANDRA. Yes.

RAY. So they'd have your records…

SANDRA. No.

Yes.

Maybe.

But sure I didn't tell them what happened.

RAY. You didn't?

SANDRA. No.

I didn't tell them.

Of course I didn't tell them.

I might have had to go to the police.

And they might have called to the house.

How could I do that to Mammy?

No. No.

I couldn't tell them.

I didn't tell them.

I just said I fell down the stairs.

Running for the phone.

A phone call.

RAY. Right.

SANDRA. So they fixed my nose.

But I've always hated it.

Haven't I.

You know how I hate my nose.

RAY. I just wish that you'd have told me.

SANDRA. How, Ray?

When, Ray?

And what would I say?

What would I?... No.

No.

I did what I had to do.

I sucked it up.

I stayed quiet.

I did my exams.

Then I went away.

I closed.

RAY. Right.

SANDRA. He raped me. They raped me, Ray.

Rape. Rape. Rape.

Rape. Rape. Ray.

Rape.

That's what it is, isn't it?

When you say no.

When you beg no.

When you...

With all your being.

With all your might... your fight...

...resist.

Fuck...

Finally... I've said it.

Beat.

RAY *stands up.*

RAY. Okay.

SANDRA. Okay?

RAY. I hear you. I understand.

SANDRA. Do you? Do you really?

RAY. Yes I do.

And we will go to the police.

If that's what you want.

SANDRA. If that's what I want?

RAY. But he swears it isn't him.

Just so you know.

He swears it isn't true.

SANDRA. It is true, Ray.

DAIRNE *enters with two small old-world electric-bar heaters.*

DAIRNE. I found these two yokes upstairs.

So I thought that if I plugged them in… it might be warmer… or I could make tea… or I could help… or I could just go home… whatever you need. Whatever you think?

SANDRA. I think… I think I need to get out of here actually.

RAY. Sandra…?

SANDRA. I think I need some air… some air, Ray… five minutes… please.

She leaves abruptly.

RAY *and* DAIRNE *are left looking at each other.*

DAIRNE. Well…

RAY. Well what?

DAIRNE. Em.

Eh.

I don't know really.

RAY. What the hell is going on?

DAIRNE. I honestly don't know…

RAY. Did you know?

Did you know about this?

(*Shouting.*) Did you know about it?!

DAIRNE. No!

RAY. But you were… she said you were…?

DAIRNE. We were friends.

Yes.

But I wasn't at that party…

At least I don't think I was!

RAY. You don't think you were?

DAIRNE. I'd have to ask her… I'd have to ask Sandra… I mean it's… it was years ago.

RAY. Do you think it's true?

DAIRNE. What?

RAY. Do you think it happened?

DAIRNE. Jesus!

RAY. He said… Eddie said and *she* said that she was drinking…

DAIRNE. This is your wife, Ray!

RAY. Exactly.

My wife.

Sandra is my wife.

DAIRNE. And you don't believe her?

RAY. I never said that… I just don't know that it was him… or that it was… I mean… there's never… she's never… and I've never had any reason to think… to feel. I mean that would affect you wouldn't it? Something like that. Rape! That would affect everything? You couldn't keep it… you couldn't just keep that down could you?

DAIRNE. People do, Ray.

People keep all kinds of shit… 'down'…

RAY. But he said.

Eddie Dunne.

He insisted it wasn't him.

DAIRNE. He's hardly likely to 'insist' on anything else now, is he?

RAY *looks at* DAIRNE.

RAY. I don't know… I'm lost, totally lost.

DAIRNE. Okay…

RAY. Because she says… Sandra says that she's going to go to the police.

DAIRNE. Does she?

RAY. Do you think that's wise?

DAIRNE. I don't know, Ray… I'm not… I'm not exactly well-versed in this kind of thing.

RAY. Well-'versed'?

DAIRNE. Well-anything!

Well-experienced!

I mean… I haven't a fucking clue…

That's what I'm trying to say.

RAY. But she has no proof.

There is no proof.

What is she going to say to the police?

DAIRNE. I don't know…

You need to ask Sandra, not me.

RAY. I love Sandra.

I love her…

DAIRNE. Well, that's good… that's important… it feels important right now.

RAY. Why did I tell you that?

Why on earth did I just tell you that?

DAIRNE. I'm not quite sure.

RAY. I don't even know you… and you're… you're actually a man.

DAIRNE. No. I'm not.

RAY. You were a man when you went out with Sandra.

DAIRNE. I wasn't. I amn't and I never went out with Sandra…

RAY. But she said… that woman… Linda… she said…

DAIRNE. Don't mind her.

She's crazy… crazed!

RAY. She said that you were 'screwing'?

DAIRNE. We weren't.

She was… Sandra was like a sister to me.

RAY. A sister! But I've never even heard of you?

I've never met you?

DAIRNE. I went away…

RAY. You went away?

DAIRNE. That's what we did then… if we…

…if you…

Ireland was a different place, wasn't it?

People… young people… people like me…

…we just went away.

RAY *puts his head in his hands*.

RAY. Fuck.

I need a drink.

He pours a gin.

DAIRNE. So do I please.

RAY *pours* DAIRNE *a gin*.

Thank you.

I don't know why I feel like I've done something wrong?

RAY. You haven't done anything wrong.

DAIRNE. No, Eddie... Eddie's the fucker that's done something wrong.

RAY. Eddie Dunne.

They drink.

But if she knew him.

If she knew who they were.

Why didn't she report it?

DAIRNE. I don't know.

I'm sure she was frightened...

RAY. He said that he is going to the police!

DAIRNE. Eddie?

RAY. Yeah! They said they were going straight to the police from here!

DAIRNE. You'll probably all meet them at the station.

RAY *puts his head in his hands*.

RAY. Jesus... I can't believe this.

DAIRNE. I can't believe this either.

I can't believe I wasn't there.

I should have been there.

She was my guardian angel.

RAY. Your what?

DAIRNE. I know it sounds corny but that's who Sandra always was to me.

RAY. An angel?

DAIRNE. She accepted me. And she was the only one around here who did. The only one to stick by... since we were kids.

RAY *pours another drink for himself.* DAIRNE *sticks out her glass.*

I think it was when we were about nine... and everything was changing... boys played with boys ... and boys played football and had fights but I still wanted to hang out with the girls. I still wanted to play their games. But that wasn't allowed so I got the shit kicked out of me every day until one sunny morning Sandra Byrne blew a gasket... Sandra Byrne walked right up to the lads in the yard and took my hand and pulled me out from under them and said, 'David's my friend so you had better leave him alone,' and she said that I was to come with her and she was beautiful so they all liked her so they left me alone. She was my armour, my protector, my angel from that day.

Makeovers.

Sleepovers.

She never left me out.

I always wanted to be just like her!

I wanted to climb inside that beautiful girl and be her, be Sandra Byrne.

Talk like her.

Laugh like her.

Walk in her espadrilles.

I modelled myself on Sandra Byrne.

Even followed her out to UCD... to London!

RAY. So where did you fucking disappear to?

I never even heard of you until tonight?

DAIRNE. I don't know...

I didn't mean to disappear but...

I don't know... we had a few crazy years in London and then I got that gig in New York.

I kind of thought she'd come over but...

And I never knew about this.

Never knew...

No one did.

Bright car headlights suddenly shine into the room.

RAY. Who the hell could that be?

Oh my God do you think it's the police?

DAIRNE. Eddie Dunne won't go to the police, Ray.

Eddie Dunne won't pull this shit down on his head.

RAY. You think?

DAIRNE. I know.

I know cowards.

RAY. So who the hell is it?

SANDRA *runs into the room.*

SANDRA. It's them!

RAY. Who?

SANDRA. Linda and him... him... they are in the drive... they are in the driveway right now...

RAY. You're joking.

SANDRA. Do I look like I'm joking? Get them out, Ray. Get them away. Please, I don't want them here.

She is shaking.

RAY *looks out the window.*

RAY. Fucking hell... it is them?

DAIRNE. I don't believe it...

EDDIE *is now standing at the window with a bandage over his head.*

SANDRA. Don't let him in.

Don't let him in!

RAY. Okay.

Okay, love.

Don't worry.

I'll handle it.

EDDIE *knocks on the window.*

DAIRNE *stands up and shouts to the window.*

DAIRNE. Fuck off!

Fuck off out of here, you bastard.

RAY *exits.*

RAY. I'll get rid of him, I promise.

As RAY *exits,* LINDA *enters from the kitchen:*

LINDA. You've got to talk to us.

SANDRA. Get out.

LINDA. No. Not until we sort this out.

DAIRNE. She doesn't want you here.

LINDA. I don't give a shit.

She can't go throwing around accusations.

SANDRA. It's not an accusation.

He knows it's true.

LINDA. Like hell he does.

DAIRNE. Do you know it's true?

LINDA. What?

DAIRNE. You heard me.

Slight pause.

LINDA. It's nonsense is what it is and I don't know what's driving it... what's driving you, Sandra, because you've been away a long time.

SANDRA. Yes I have.

I've been away a long time.

LINDA. And this is fucking serious.

SANDRA. I know it's serious, Linda...

LINDA. Because this isn't only Eddie you're fucking with. This is me... and my life... and my daughters' lives... have you thought about that?

SANDRA. What?

LINDA. My daughters are in third class.

And my daughters love their daddy.

And my daughters are two great kids.

And if this gets out... if even a hint of this... this shit you're spouting leaves this room... then their life, their home, their world collapses... it collapses, Sandra... and I know you know that.

I know you understand that.

SANDRA. Don't... don't lay that on me...

LINDA. They are nine years old.

SANDRA. I said... don't lay that on me, Linda!

LINDA. And you are a mother yourself...

DAIRNE. You bitch.

LINDA. This... You... you will destroy their life.

SANDRA. I have... I have no intention...

I have nothing against them or you.

LINDA. Then bury this.

Stop this.

Stop it now.

SANDRA. But it has been 'buried' too long...

LINDA. And it hasn't done you any harm, has it?

SANDRA *gasps*.

I mean you have a life.

You have a husband.

Children.

You're on your feet.

You're grand.

SANDRA. Jesus... Jesus Christ... you have no idea what this
has done to me!

LINDA. If you go public with this, you will destroy us!

SANDRA. No, he destroys you, Linda! He does. Not me.

It is *his* deceit. Your husband's deceit.

And his violence.

DAIRNE. And his arrogance.

SANDRA. Yes and his fucking arrogance...

LINDA. No, no, you don't know him.

SANDRA. His surety that it, that I would never have the courage to challenge him.

DAIRNE. But now you've found the courage.

SANDRA. Yes I have.

I have, Dairne. I mean I never imagined...

I had no notion that you married that bastard, or that you would bring him here.

To my house... to my parents' house!

So what do you expect me to do?

LINDA. I expect, I expect you to do what's right for your family... and for my family...

SANDRA. But what about me?

LINDA. You! You just need to listen to resaon... to Eddie... because he says... he swears... he wasn't on Rathmines Road!

DAIRNE. We all went to parties on Rathmines Road...

LINDA. Exactly!

So it could have been anyone!

On any night!

SANDRA. I wasn't raped on any night, Linda.

It was April 16th 1993.

April 16th at Áine Doyle's flat.

498 Rathmines Road.

By Eddie Dunne and Jay Blake.

LINDA. So did you report it?

 Did you get witnesses?

 Did you go to a centre… a hospital?

SANDRA. No.

LINDA. No!

SANDRA. No.

LINDA. Then it's just your word.

SANDRA. Yes, it's just my word.

LINDA. On a drunken night.

 At a student party.

 Over twenty years ago.

 Ridiculous.

 RAY *enters. He sees* LINDA.

RAY. What's SHE doing here?

DAIRNE. She came in the back door.

RAY. This is bloody harassment!

 EDDIE *enters*.

LINDA. You started all this!

EDDIE. I think we all need to calm down.

RAY. I told you to leave!

 He starts trying to push EDDIE *out the door.* EDDIE *pushes back*.

EDDIE. Not until we sort this out.

LINDA. Don't leave, Eddie.

SANDRA. Get him out, Ray.

DAIRNE. You're not wanted here.

LINDA. We stay until it's sorted...!

EDDIE. You have to realise... it wasn't me!

SANDRA. So look me in the face and say that.

Look me straight in the face.

And say that you didn't rape me.

EDDIE *and* RAY *stop pushing.*

EDDIE *straightens himself.*

EDDIE. Thank you. Thank you, Sandra.

For the opportunity.

We have an opportunity to clear this up.

SANDRA. Just say it.

EDDIE. I'm so sorry. I am incredibly sorry that this happened to you.

It's... it's a terrible thing.

A total betrayal by...

SANDRA. Donal.

Donal Mooney.

A friend of yours.

EDDIE. No...

SANDRA. He's not a friend of yours?

LINDA. We used to know him.

EDDIE. We used to know him.

SANDRA. And Jay Blake?

EDDIE. I knew Jay. I knew a lot of people but that doesn't mean that I was at that party and that doesn't mean that I would do... do what you described... to anyone...

SANDRA. When I went to London first.

I used to drink myself stupid.

I used to sleep with my passport and a kitchen knife under my pillow.

I was always ready to run, Eddie Dunne.

Run far.

Run further.

And I used to jump if anyone moved within yards of me.

I was terrified most of the time… all of the time.

And I hated myself.

Hated what I had allowed happen to me.

And I thought I would never pull myself out of that place… but I did.

With writing.

With counselling.

With work.

And with Ray.

RAY. Please, love…

SANDRA. It took years. Years… to find a part of myself that was still strong… still young and still intact, mostly thanks to Ray.

So I could build… I built from there.

And I built someone else.

Not the girl you left at that party.

Not the girl you left on the floor.

EDDIE. Right.

Okay…

SANDRA. Did you ever think about me?

> After?

EDDIE. Look. Sandra.

> *She winces.*

> I remember Donal. I remember him well.

> And I remember he was a bit of a 'player'…

SANDRA. Is that what you'd call it…

EDDIE. You know what I mean… come on.

> You know.

> He was a ladies' man.

SANDRA. And you weren't were you, Eddie?

EDDIE. I wasn't…

SANDRA. You were just a sidekick if I remember.

> A runt.

> Runt of the pack.

> Not so rich.

> Not so clever.

> Not the playboy.

> So did that make you feel big then, did it?

> What you did to me?

EDDIE. Look, this is crazy.

> This is… you've got to be reasonable.

> You've got the wrong guy.

SANDRA. So say it.

> Say it to me.

> 'I didn't touch you.'

'I didn't hurt you.'

'I didn't rape you.'

He looks her in the eye.

EDDIE. I didn't… rape… you.

SANDRA. You're worse that I thought.

Beat.

LINDA. Okay

Okay… you've had your fun now.

You've had your twisted fucking… whatever now.

Eddie's made it clear…

So I want to know.

We need to know.

That THIS… this –

EDDIE. Mix-up.

LINDA. This mix-up… won't leave this room.

RAY. 'Mix-up'?

EDDIE. I have a career, Ray.

I have a family.

DAIRNE. Ah! The career.

That's all he really cares about, Sandra.

LINDA. Why don't you stay out of it!

DAIRNE. Why don't you stay out of it!

LINDA. Because this is my life!

DAIRNE. And Sandra is my friend!

LINDA. Hah! (*Laughs.*)

Would you listen to that!

'*Sandra is my friend!*'

DAIRNE. She is. She was. So I should have been there.

I wish I'd been there.

I wish I'd helped.

Why didn't you tell me, Sandra?

SANDRA. For Christ's sake.

DAIRNE. You were the world to me.

SANDRA. No I wasn't.

Not then.

You'd found your own crowd.

And I was glad for you...

You were living your own life.

LINDA. You bet he was.

Living his own life.

So why would he give a shit about you?

That's a lifetime of preconditioning right there.

Years of being a man so tits or no tits the world still revolves around you!

DAIRNE. You have no right to say that!

LINDA. Haven't I?

DAIRNE. You have no right to undermine me.

You don't even know me!

LINDA. I know MEN.

EDDIE. This isn't helpful, Linda.

LINDA. Oh shut the fuck up, Eddie. I'm sick of it.

Sick of the lot of you... and now this!

This... 'I used to be David, now I'm Dairne.'

The dick is gone so give me your heels!

Well, fuck you!

EDDIE. Please, Linda…!

LINDA. No. No way! You've got to earn these stripes, Dairne.

DAIRNE. I've earned them.

LINDA. I don't think so. You haven't sucked it up, have you?…
Over years, have you? The leers, the jeers, the quiet
condescension or the simply blatant shit. You haven't been
groped, Dairne… poked, and pushed and letched. Has he,
Sandra? Tell him, Sandra, tell him what it's like to live with
these beauties since you were ten years old? Melon tits. Milk
jugs. I've been scarlet, haven't you, Sandra?… I've been
scarlet since life on the skipping rope! Because men whisper
in your ear… when you're a kid… old men… young men…
strange men… at bus stops, at the shops, at fucking mass!
'Open those legs… legs wide open!' 'Give us a feel!'

You're a target, just by virtue of this – (*Indicates her body.*)
Just like Sandra was a target… if she was a target that
night… at that party… and I'm sure she was… because it
happened… happens… and it has happened to me plenty…
because I look good and I like sex… *liked* sex… disaster…
that doesn't work for girls, Dairne… real girls… not in
Glenealy anyway… because you get a name… you get
labelled and then… guess what… you're ripe for the picking
because you're dirt… you're easy… you're just a whore
anyway. And you think you'll never survive it… like Sandra
thought she'd never survive it but you do… coz you're bred
to survive it. That's years of genetic genius right there…
right here… (*Pointing to herself.*) It's like evolution only
seems to work one way… BUT I'm not sucking this up, I'm
not having my life fucked up again by YOU or YOU or YOU
or anyone else.

Got it?!

DAIRNE. I understand what you are saying.

LINDA. No you don't.

DAIRNE. I've been spat at, ridiculed, punched and buggered, Linda. All because I refuse… All because I feel… I know… that I am a woman like you.

EDDIE. I think we're getting a little off-point here.

RAY. Off-point?

LINDA. We need to be clear.

EDDIE. Yes we do.

Clear.

But not emotional, Linda.

LINDA. Jesus! Do you hear that?

I'm emotional.

But I'm not to *be* emotional.

Forget the fact that she's just said my husband is a rapist!

EDDIE. You're not helping! This is not helping!

LINDA. I am, Eddie. Once again I am helping… so what I am going to do to 'help' this time is I'm going to sell Sandra's house. I'm going to sell it quicker and for more money than she could have ever dreamed of. And then Sandra… You!… We!… We will never set eyes on each other or our families again.

Okay?

Okay, Ray?

RAY. There is…

There is nothing 'okay' about this.

SANDRA. No.

Nothing.

DAIRNE. Nothing.

EDDIE. Then let me appeal to reason, Ray.

LINDA. I…

EDDIE. Linda… stop. Just stop. You're making everything worse. I need to talk to Ray. Man to man.

LINDA. Oh for fuck's sake…

EDDIE. I need to appeal…!

I need to appeal to you, Ray.

To your reason.

Because…

I know…

I know you must be… you are… a reasonable man… and I know that you know that there's nothing to be gained by pursuing this.

Because…

There is no way to prove it ever happened.

The police will ask a series of embarrassing…

LINDA. Invasive…!

EDDIE. Invasive questions. And…

Our families will get dragged into it.

Our reputations… private and professional. And we will all be deeply compromised. All of us.

DAIRNE. That is such bollox.

RAY. You two are unbelievable.

EDDIE. No. No, Ray.

We are just pointing out what is fact here…

RAY. But what is 'fact' here?

That's what I want to know.

What is fact?

Did you do it?

Did you do that to Sandra?

My wife?

EDDIE. Noooo… No.

SANDRA. And that's why I ran away.

But you know that don't you, Eddie.

Of course you know that.

Because no one would listen.

No one would believe…

They never believe… do they?

And just look at you!

Look at him, Ray.

The voice of reason.

The voice of respectability.

In his V-neck.

And his Chinos.

The decent man.

He's even a teacher, for fuck's sake!

EDDIE. I am a decent man!

I am not that guy at the party.

SANDRA. Aren't you?

She goes over to him.

You put your hands on me.

When I asked you not to.

Told you not to.

You grabbed my shoulders here.

You tore my skin right here.

You bit me.

And you remember.

I know you remember.

You stole a part of me… when you raped me.

He is affected by this.

EDDIE. Lots of people have sex at parties.

DAIRNE. Did you do it more than once, Eddie?

EDDIE. Lots of people have sex at parties.

SANDRA. Did you do it to a lot of girls?

Keep score?

Notch it up?

EDDIE. No!

No.

SANDRA. I never said 'yes'.

I never wanted you.

LINDA. There is nothing.

Nothing to be gained by going public with this.

You will destroy yourself.

SANDRA. I will destroy myself?

DAIRNE. Don't listen to her, Sandra.

LINDA. It's too late.

DAIRNE. It's never too late for the truth.

EDDIE. Look, if you persist… if you pursue… well… it could
have serious consequences.

DAIRNE. For who, Eddie?

EDDIE. You need to protect your family. Your name.

LINDA. Because this is a small town.

SANDRA. But I don't care that it's a small town, Linda.

I don't care any more.

I'm an adult now.

I'm a big girl.

Not that girl you tossed on the floor.

LINDA. But what about Ray?

SANDRA. What?

LINDA. You don't want to do this to Ray.

Or to your children.

SANDRA. What?

LINDA. Drag this dirt into their life.

SANDRA. Stop!

RAY. Yes stop.

Stop this right away…

LINDA. So what do you want?

SANDRA. Want?

LINDA. Is it money?

DAIRNE. Oh my God…

EDDIE. Linda!

SANDRA. I want him to admit it.

LINDA. You want him to admit it? And if he does?

EDDIE. If he what?

LINDA. If he does?

Will you go back to London?

And will you swear that this... that this conversation never leaves this room?

EDDIE. Don't be an idiot, Linda.

LINDA. And don't you be an idiot, Eddie.

This is damage limitation.

Think of the girls.

SANDRA. Yes, think of your girls, Eddie Dunne.

Think of your daughters.

Imagine some bastard did to one of them what you did to me.

EDDIE. Don't talk about my daughters.

SANDRA. Why?

EDDIE. Because they are nothing like you...!

SANDRA. Why?

What am I?

EDDIE. I love my daughters.

SANDRA. And your love makes them special, does it?

Your love is more important than mine?

YOU are more important?

DAIRNE. Why don't you just admit it, you bastard.

EDDIE. Because it's not true.

DAIRNE. Do you hate the guy at the party, Ed?

Do you hate who you used to be?

LINDA. Why don't you shut up.

DAIRNE. Why don't you shut up!

RAY. Stop it.

   Stop this.

   I've asked you all to stop.

LINDA. See! Look what you're doing to Ray!

DAIRNE. Go on! Admit it.

SANDRA. That might be justice enough for me.

LINDA. Okay... okay then, he'll admit it.

EDDIE. What?

LINDA. If that's all she wants... fucking admit it and we can all
   go home.

EDDIE. Are you serious!

LINDA. Yes I'm serious. I'm warning you... I don't... I don't
   want Dad or the family or my daughters brought into this.
   This... This... is your mess. It's always your mess, Eddie.
   And I'm not pulling you out any more.

EDDIE. All right.

   All right.

   If that's what...

   If that's what you 'need'.

   Maybe...

   Maybe there was a night.

SANDRA. On Rathmines Road.

EDDIE. On Rathmines Road.

SANDRA. When you followed a girl.

EDDIE. When I followed a girl.

SANDRA. Into a room.

EDDIE. Into a room.

SANDRA. And watched her.

EDDIE. Watched…

SANDRA. And tricked her.

And forced her.

He shakes his head.

EDDIE. It was just sex.

And you were up for it.

She was up for it.

SANDRA. I wasn't 'up for it'.

EDDIE. So you should have said.

SANDRA. I did say.

I did say.

The music from the party returns.

EDDIE. That's not how I remember it.

SANDRA. But you do remember?

EDDIE. I didn't sleep with a lot of girls.

SANDRA. You didn't 'sleep' with me.

EDDIE. Maybe not.

Maybe it was rough.

Rougher than I remember.

Maybe you did say no.

SANDRA. I did.

I said 'No'.

Over and over.

EDDIE. But…

SANDRA. But what?

The music stops.

Say it.

Say it, Eddie Dunne, because I need to believe,

I need to believe what I remember.

I need to believe ME.

EDDIE. I'm sorry.

I apologise.

I wasn't aware... I wasn't aware of of the pain caused...

SANDRA. What?

DAIRNE. What's that supposed to be?

EDDIE. An apology! It's an apology!

LINDA. There you go, he has apologised.

DAIRNE. Fucking abysmal...

SANDRA. Not enough.

DAIRNE. Too right it's not enough.

SANDRA. I need you to own it.

To understand what you did to me.

To my life.

To my person.

EDDIE. There are some things... some... events, moments, decisions... that I'm not proud of...

SANDRA. Is that what I am?

An event?

EDDIE. I am trying...

It's just not that simple...

DAIRNE. It is actually.

It is simple.

EDDIE. Maybe I do remember.

LINDA. So you do remember!

EDDIE. Something… Something!… but it's not like she describes.

No, it's not like she describes…

I thought… I mean she was really drunk!

You were really drunk!

SANDRA. So?

EDDIE. And yes, we knew your crowd…

And I was drunk. A little.

And I was tired of being… you're right… right about that. I was on the fringes.

I was not… I was not who I wanted to be.

And you… you and Donal…

When you were dancing.

Well, it was like a show!

It was like you were putting on a show on the dance floor.

And he had.

He was all over you, Donal…

And.

And him and Jay… they used to…

They did this…

I knew they did this…

They bragged about it.

They said that girls loved it…

They said that girls agreed…

So…

So I followed them into the room.

To the bedroom.

Like you said.

And we watched you and Donal… at it.

And then when he was finished.

When you were finished.

Well…

It didn't…

I didn't think it was…

What you say it is.

And you were so drunk…

I mean really.

To the others.

You should have seen her…

She was falling all over the place.

DAIRNE. Absolute scumbag.

SANDRA. Oh my God.

Oh my God.

RAY. You did… You did…

SANDRA. It so fucking wasn't okay

It so fucking wasn't…

Beat.

EDDIE. But I didn't know that I broke your nose.

I'm sorry I broke your nose.

And I, I never felt very good about that night.

What happened.

I didn't enjoy it.

If that helps.

If that's any help.

DAIRNE. Jesus.

EDDIE. And I never... I never ever participated again.

Because I'm not that sort of man.

Am I, Linda?

I'm not that sort of man.

LINDA *doesn't respond*.

SANDRA. But you are, Eddie Dunne.

Beat.

RAY. Can you leave now.

Can you two fucking leave please before I kill you.

LINDA. Not unless you promise.

Not unless she promises...

I'm not asking for me, Sandra.

I'm asking for my girls.

Don't turn their father into a rapist.

RAY *stands up... threatening*.

RAY. What do I need to do?

What is it I need to do?

EDDIE. Okay. Okay. We will go.

And we can talk again in the morning?

How about that?

RAY. NO!

LINDA. I'll fight you all the way.

Fight this all the way.

DAIRNE. Even when you know he did it, Linda…?

LINDA. What do you know? What do you know? Fucking nothing is what. This will stick, Sandra. Stick to me and my kids… and tear at us… destroy us but then you know that… of course you know that… that's why you never reported it in the first place. That's why you went away.

EDDIE. Come on, Linda.

LINDA. But you'll destroy yourself too… if you do this.

And you'll destroy your marriage.

He'll never look at you in the same way.

Will he?

Will you, Ray?

RAY. Get out.

For the love of God GET OUT.

EDDIE. Linda!

He goes to grab her arm.

LINDA. Don't…

Don't fucking touch me.

They are gone.

SANDRA *sits.*

DAIRNE. Now lock all the fucking doors!

SANDRA *laughs*.

DAIRNE *laughs*.

RAY. Are you laughing?

Are you actually laughing?

DAIRNE. Not really.

SANDRA. No.

Not really

RAY. I think. I think I am going to be sick.

Excuse me…

SANDRA. Ray?!

RAY. Excuse me.

He is gone.

SANDRA. Jesus –

DAIRNE. Wept!

SANDRA. Yes he did.

Yes he did.

He wept.

DAIRNE. They are something else.

Aren't they?

That pair.

Something else.

Slight pause.

Is that true – what you said about the passport?

The knife?

SANDRA. Of course it's true.

It's all fucking true, Dairne.

DAIRNE. How did I not know?

SANDRA. It doesn't matter.

DAIRNE. It matters to me.

Those two years in London… it looked like you were having a ball!

SANDRA. I wasn't. I was having a breakdown.

DAIRNE. Fuck.

SANDRA. Yes.

But I'm okay now.

I've got Ray.

I've got my kids.

And they are my focus.

DAIRNE. Of course they are.

SANDRA. So I want to go and talk to Ray, Dairne.

DAIRNE. Sure.

I'll go…

SANDRA. Because I can't lose him.

DAIRNE. You won't lose him.

SANDRA. Did you see his face?

DAIRNE. Shock.

It's just a shock.

SANDRA. I hope so.

DAIRNE. He'll know.

He knows that you're still the same person, Sandra.

Still that same girl.

SANDRA. Oh God…

DAIRNE. What!

SANDRA. Maybe I have destroyed everything… Just like Linda said.

DAIRNE. Stop.

Don't doubt yourself.

That's what they want.

You have to hold on to the truth.

You have to hold on to it.

RAY *returns*.

SANDRA. Ray?

RAY*'s head is down*.

Are you okay?

RAY. Yes. Yeah. I'm okay.

DAIRNE. I'm going to leave now.

I'm going…

I'll be… I'll just be up in Mammy's.

For tonight… tomorrow.

If you need anything… Sandra.

If you need anything…

SANDRA. Okay.

RAY. Yes.

Eh thanks, Dairne.

DAIRNE *hugs* SANDRA.

DAIRNE (*quietly*). Hold it, Sandra, hold on to it.

She stands opposite RAY. *They are awkward. They just shake hands.*

Goodnight… Ray.

RAY. Goodnight.

She exits.

The two stand in the living room.

SANDRA. Are you feeling better?

RAY. No.

SANDRA. Oh God, it doesn't change anything, does it?

It doesn't change us?

RAY. Of course it doesn't change us.

SANDRA. But I'm afraid that you won't love me now.

Don't love me now.

RAY. How can you say that?

After... after everything... after the kids...?

Jesus...

SANDRA. No... no... please.

I don't doubt you.

RAY. But you do.

You obviously do.

Because you never told me... and I... I thought we shared everything?

I thought we were everything?

SANDRA. We are.

RAY. Then I don't understand... I can't understand...

WHY?

I mean is it me?

Is it my fault?

That you thought you couldn't tell me?

SANDRA. No, no of course not.

RAY. Then why?

SANDRA. Because… because how, Ray?

How?

And when?

When is a good time to open up that sore?

When we were dating?

When you asked me to marry you?

It felt, it feels like a curse, Ray.

It has always felt like a curse, like pus.

And it's septic. Toxic. She's right, Linda Levins.

She's right about that. It sticks. Rape sticks.

Once you say it, acknowledge it.

And that is why I went away.

And that was the right thing to do because then I found you. I found you, Ray.

And I wanted you.

I wanted you so much.

And I wanted.

I want!

Our happiness.

Our love.

And why shouldn't I, Ray?

Why should I stay tied to that night on Rathmines Road?

RAY. But I would never judge you.

SANDRA. Wouldn't you?

RAY. No.

How can you even think that?

SANDRA. Because you made me feel good again, Ray.

And when I thought that wasn't possible.

In a pure… in that pure way… and not feel…

…not hate myself.

RAY. Oh God…!

SANDRA. What?

RAY. I didn't know!

I didn't know that that had happened to you.

SANDRA. It doesn't matter.

RAY. But of course it does.

Of course it does.

When we were together… when we were together, Sandra,
I thought it was just us.

SANDRA. It was just us.

Of course it was just us.

RAY. Was it?

Or was it shadowed?

Please be honest with me, Sandra.

Our moments?

Our intimacy?

Was it shadowed by him?

SANDRA. No!

RAY. By them?

By that night?

SANDRA. No. No. Ray.

I swear.

RAY. Never?

She doesn't answer.

Never?

SANDRA. No, not never.

RAY. Christ!

SANDRA. But only at the beginning.

Maybe at the beginning?

I was nervous… I was so fucked up, Ray… I was frightened…

RAY. Frightened of me?

SANDRA. No, no… you made me feel safe.

Pause.

RAY. It's late.

It's very late.

It's so late.

And it's been… it's been a kind of cataclysmic night, Sandra.

SANDRA. Cataclysmic?

Cataclysmic? What the fuck is that?

RAY. I need to go to bed.

I really think we just need to go to bed.

Because I can't… I can't talk any more. Okay.

SANDRA. Why?

RAY. Because… because, Sandra.

Now everything… everything is starting to feel like a lie.

SANDRA. No. No. No.

Don't say that.

You can't say that.

We're not a lie.

Séan and Emma are not a lie…

He is visibly distressed.

RAY. Jesus Christ… the kids.

SANDRA. This changes nothing, Ray.

I'm still the same person.

I love Séan and Emma.

RAY. But do you trust me, Sandra?

SANDRA. I trust you. Of course I trust you.

I trust you with every inch.

Every inch of me, Ray.

Inside and out.

And do you know?

Can you ever know?

The courage.

The love.

The love that that took from me.

He shakes his head.

RAY. I thought I did.

I thought I knew you.

SANDRA. Nothing has changed.

Nothing has changed.

SANDRA *looks at* RAY, *terrified.*

Beat.

Lighting and music return.

She doesn't move. We only see her in a spot, just like page 52.

I can't do it.

I can't.

I will destroy everything.

I will destroy everything if I...

Slight pause.

I must... I'll just...

I'll close my eyes.

Close my eyes all over again.

Because I can't win.

I can't...

If I lose Ray, I'll lose me.

And I don't have the strength.

I don't have the strength to start again.

I'll just

Close... my eyes.

The music and lighting stops...

SANDRA *sits back on the couch.*

RAY *enters and sits next to her.*

Scene Four

She holds his face. She starts to kiss his face.

SANDRA. You are everything. Everything. To me.

The kissing becomes more passionate.

I love you.

I love you.

You know that don't you. I love you.

They start to make love. The lighting and music are loud and frenetic over their love-making. They stop. They are entwined.

RAY. God... I'm getting too old for this!

SANDRA. No you're not. You're amazing.

RAY. No you're amazing.

SANDRA. You know I love you, don't you, Ray.

You know I love you more than anything.

You and Séan and Emma. You are everything to me.

Everything.

EVERYTHING.

RAY. Who are you shouting at?

SANDRA. I don't know.

Everyone maybe.

Everything.

RAY. Are you sure you're all right?

SANDRA. Yes.

RAY. Are you crying?

SANDRA. No.

RAY. Are you sure… you look like you're crying?

SANDRA. No I'm not… I'm fine. I'm honestly fine.

RAY. Okay. But what was going on with you this evening?

SANDRA. What?

RAY. When the others were here?

SANDRA. Nothing!

RAY. Nothing?

SANDRA. Do you mind moving… I just want to fix my dress.

> RAY *moves and keeps going with the opening scene exactly
> as at the top of the play but we don't hear them any more, we
> just see the exact same movements and expressions as the
> music rolls in and the lights fade.*
>
> *End.*

A Nick Hern Book

Rathmines Road first published in Great Britain in 2018 as a paperback original by Nick Hern Books Limited, The Glasshouse, 49a Goldhawk Road, London W12 8QP, in association with Fishamble Theatre Company and the Abbey Theatre, Dublin

Rathmines Road © 2018 Deirdre Kinahan

Deirdre Kinahan has asserted her moral right to be identified as the author of this work

Cover photograph of Janet Moran, Charlie Bonner, Karen Ardiff, Enda Oates and Rebecca Root by Patrick Redmond

Designed and typeset by Nick Hern Books, London
Printed in Great Britain by Mimeo Ltd, Huntingdon, Cambridgeshire PE29 6XX

A CIP catalogue record for this book is available from the British Library

ISBN 978 1 84842 777 8

Woodland
CARBON
www.woodlandcarbon.co.uk
NICK HERN BOOKS
Printed on Carbon Captured paper